For Anne and Graha
First of all, thank you
Coming to my presentat...
Thank you both for your interest in my story.
May you both enjoy reading it and may
it fill you with emotion and make you want

Survivor, Scientist, Olympian:
The Nary Ly Story

How a Child of the Killing Fields Ran an Olympic Marathon
and Inspired Her Broken Nation

to travel the world!

My sincere wishes of happiness and health.

By Nary LY

cazenovia, 22 oct 2022

Cover design and book layout: Francisco A. Morais
moraisf@gmail.com

Olympic Games photo credit: EFE/EPA/Diego Azubel

Copyrights © 2019 Nary Ly

Legal deposit: LE 325-2020

ISBN: 978-84-09-21435-8

First printing edition, 2020 in Spain

www.facebook.com/narylyauthor

naryly@gmail.com

"Science knows no country, because knowledge belongs to humanity, and is the torch which illuminates the world."

Louis Pasteur
French biologist, microbiologist and chemist, 1822-1895

"Olympism seeks to create a way of life based on the joy found in effort, the educational value of a good example and respect for universal fundamental ethical principles."

Pierre de Coubertin
French educator and historian,
and founder of the International Olympic Committee, 1863-1937

In memory of all the innocent victims of the Khmer Rouge.

To my Cambodian and French families and especially my sister Heang.

To my friends.

Table of Contents

Prologue - Summer Olympics, Rio de Janeiro..................1

Historical Note..................5

Part One: Cambodia..................7

1 - Crickets and Flower Bud Games: My Early Childhood..................9

2 - A Childhood Stolen: The Khmer Rouge Years..................17

3 - Rescue..................25

Part Two: France..................35

4 - Becoming a French Girl..................37

5 - Headstrong: Taking Control of My Life..................49

6 - Keeping on Track in a Tough Foster Hostel..................63

Part Three: Back to my Roots..................77

7 - Reunion with My Lost Family..................79

8 - A Year in - and for - Cambodia..................89

Part Four: Becoming a Scientist-and Athlete..................111

9 - Hitting the Books to Earn a PhD..................113

10 - New York: Mount Sinai and My First Marathon..................129

Part Five: A Khmer Rouge Survivor's Revenge..................155

11 - Cambodian National Athlete, Training at the Home of Champions..................157

12 - Out of Money but Not Motivation..................171

13 - Tracking Mystery Diseases in Cambodia..................187

14 - A Last Attempt at My Running Goals..................193

Part Six: Inspiring the Next Generation..................207

15 - A Marathon in Under 3 Hours..................209

16 - Getting Nominated for the Olympic Games..................221

17 - Summer Olympics: 26 Miles in the Blazing Heat of Rio..................229

18 - Life After the Olympics..................241

Epilogue..................245

Acknowledgments..................251

Note..................253

About the author..................255

-Prologue-
Summer Olympics, Rio de Janeiro

So here it was—my day to line up to run the marathon at the 2016 Summer Olympics in Rio de Janeiro. It was my privilege to be the first-ever Cambodian female marathoner to stand under the start arch of this great event. Through me, my small and impoverished country, still struggling to recover from a 1970s genocide, was going to compete as an equal alongside the greatest and richest countries of the world.

Standing at the back of the assembled runners, I was more than a bit nervous picturing the 26.2 miles ahead. My imagination kept conjuring up risks—injury, dehydration—that could lie ahead on the course, which wound through the streets of Rio and along its famous beach.

The day was crazy hot, humid and stifling. I kept reassuring myself that my training had been good, that only positive things would happen as long as I reached the finish line!

Against booming music and the cheers of a euphoric crowd, the countdown began.

And then the gun went off!

#

I am a survivor of genocide. At the age of five, I was torn away from my family by the Khmer Rouge fanatics who took control of my county in 1975. I was sent to work in a squalid children's labor camp. In 1981, I became an orphan refugee child in France, one of a quarter million Cambodians who were resettled in foreign countries. As a young adult I earned a PhD in biology and medical sciences and became infatuated with, of all things, running.

There is no tradition of long-distance running in my country, certainly not by women, and it's a very difficult place in which to train, what with polluted air, roads that are clogged with cars and motorbikes, and scant government support for amateur athletes. But it appealed, I think, to something innate in me, a determination to overcome obstacles, whether they're psychological or physical. Long distance running certainly has both kinds, and so did many of the other trials that my life dealt up.

Though I was fortunate to have been able to escape abroad after the genocide, as an adult I felt drawn back to my country of birth. I wanted to play a role in its recovery. Toward that end, I worked in Cambodia in a medical laboratory, conducted research into infectious diseases, taught at the National University of Health and Sciences of Cambodia, and volunteered at non-profits. It was only gradually that I conceived of another way that I might help my once-broken country return proudly to the community of nations—I would run the Olympic marathon.

#

These many disparate acts and events come together as the story I will tell in the following pages. I wrote the book, I will admit, in part for myself. I hoped that sitting down at a keyboard daily would help me achieve a sense of peace and equilibrium after a life of often devastating turmoil. Finding the right words was harder than I thought. When I first started writing, I often ended up crying. Once I had written something down, I couldn't read it again to edit it. But as I recorded more and more of my story, I found ways to take control of this feeling. I learned to examine past events without being overwhelmed by them.

It is one thing to write for yourself and quite another to write for anyone who cares to open these pages. When I was working on the book, I often felt vulnerable knowing that I would be sharing so much with strangers. Yet I came to realize that these strangers were really the prime reason for writing.

The book is coming out at a time when American and European political leaders are increasingly closing the door to migrants and refugees. I'll be thankful if some of my stranger-readers see my story as a real-life rebuttal of those cruel policies. I am proof that welcoming distressed outsiders is both an admirable act of humanity and an investment in the future. We can pick ourselves up and move beyond our traumatic pasts—the word "refugee" should not sound ugly anymore.

I will be forever grateful that France took me in after the Khmer Rouge horrors and gave me an advanced scientific education. And yet I know that the relationship has not been one-sided. I have repaid France by conducting research into AIDS and other infectious diseases, not to mention paying taxes and being a responsible member of society.

Other support has come from myriad people with whom my life has intersected—my Cambodian birth family, my French foster family, professors, coaches, fellow athletes, friends, co-workers. Each helped give me strength and perspective to become the person I am today.

Ultimately I hope that my story might serve as an example, even an inspiration, to girls and women, who in every country face special challenges in life. There could be particular relevance to those in my own country, Cambodia, which even forty years after the genocide is still struggling to advance and put those times behind it.

In recent years, I've often sat down with students and recounted my story. The best outcome that I can imagine for this book will be that it will kindle in readers a feeling that I sometimes sense in those young people, on whose shoulders rests the future of the world. They look at me as I speak, and I feel I can read their thoughts: if she can achieve her dreams, maybe I can too.

It's an amazing gift to be able to inspire others.

—Nary Ly, August 2018.

-Historical Note-

From 1975 to 1979, Cambodia was ruled by the Khmer Rouge, a regime that perpetrated one of the most horrific genocides in history.

The country had been a great power and font of civilization in ancient times, builder of the fabled temples of Angkor. But in the modern age, it fell on hard times. The French took colonial control, and many Cambodian nationalists had to flee abroad, afraid of retribution in their own country. After World War II, with French power waning, King Norodom Sihanouk successfully negotiated for independence, but more troubles lay ahead.

In the 1960s, communist groups gained influence. Full-scale war broke out in 1970 between them and an American-supported government in the capital Phnom Penh. Some historians believe that factors pushing the Khmer Rouge towards the hard left included the intense American bombing that followed. In 1975, the Khmer Rouge triumphed. Pol Pot, supreme leader of the Communist Party of Kampuchea, took control of the country. Thus was born the infamous Khmer Rouge dictatorship.

His regime was xenophobic, isolationist and horrifyingly brutal. Its goal was to re-establish Cambodia from "Year Zero." The cities were cleared, their people forced into grueling labor in the countryside. The regime was fanatically anti-intellectual, targeting professionals and university graduates, and even people who wore glasses or spoke other languages. Former city dwellers, inexperienced with farm life, often faced accusations of "economic sabotage" when they fell behind in their work, and were executed. Exploiting the Cambodian fear that their nation would disappear (as it almost did in past times under Vietnamese and Thai intervention), the Khmer Rouge also targeted people of Chinese and Vietnamese descent living in Cambodia— particularly the Vietnamese.

We don't know the full death toll. More than 20,000 mass graves have been found. The Documentation Center of Cambodia believes that the most likely figure is 2.2 million—about 30 percent of the entire population. Probably about 1.4 million of those people were executed. The rest died of starvation and disease due to the horrific living conditions.

In late 1978, Vietnam invaded and soon overthrew the Khmer Rouge. In the chaos that followed, huge numbers of Cambodians fled to refugee camps in Thailand and Vietnam. Close to a quarter million eventually went on to new lives in third countries such as France and the United States.

But the fall of the Khmer Rouge did not restore peace in Cambodia. A bloody civil war soon broke out, pitting the new government in the capital Phnom Penh against Khmer Rouge remnants and anti-communist resistance groups. Fighting continued until 1991 when the sides signed a peace agreement. The United Nations sent in a large peacekeeping force to secure the country and oversee a national election.

Cambodia has remained largely at peace since then. But corruption, authoritarian government, war damage and the genocide's virtual eradication of the educated class have combined to keep the country among the world's poorest. The 16 million people who inhabit Cambodia today continue to struggle for the prosperity that they so deeply deserve after the many years of war and brutality.

—Part One—

Cambodia

-1-
Crickets and Flower Bud Games:
My Early Childhood

I used to think I had little memory of my childhood, either of the peaceful times before the war reached my village, or the great hardships that followed. Perhaps I was simply too young to remember, or I suppressed memories. Some members of my family say I had severe nightmares when I was a child, but I do not recall them at all. However, as I wrote this book, I started to remember more and more of the things that happened in my childhood. Talks with close family members helped bring those events and feelings out of the mist, and I present them to you here in the best way I can.

My parents were both born in Cambodia, but there is some Chinese in my background: my grandmother on my mother's side and my grandfather on my father's side both came from China. Chinese people had been migrating to Cambodia for centuries, and it's not so rare to find that they are some of your ancestors.

My mother (in Cambodian, we say "Ma") was illiterate, but my father ("Pa") received a good Chinese education. They wed in 1949 when Pa was 22, and Ma was 20, through an arranged marriage. My siblings would have arranged marriages, too, and it would have been the same for me had times been normal and I had remained in Cambodia.

My parents' marriage came about because of political turmoil that was shaking the country. In the 1940s and 50s, when Cambodia was still a French colony, a group known as the Khmer Issarak was demanding independence and there was periodic violence. Soldiers sometimes kidnapped beautiful village women and forced them into marriage, or raped them. This would probably have happened to my mother, but she was sent to another village to hide with her grandmother.

That's where Ma and Pa met. The story is that Pa's aunty visited my great-grandmother, and my mother served them tea. Impressed by my mother's beauty and demeanour, my father's aunty arranged the marriage between my parents, to further protect my mother from being kidnapped.

My parents lived in Kampong Phnom, a city about fifty kilometers from the capital, Phnom Penh. Pa's family owned a small shop—he came from a line of tradespeople. Outside it, he planted vegetables. Ma took care of the house and children.

There were quite a few of us. I am the youngest of seven children whom I know of. Others might have died before I was born—I can't be sure. By the time my mother had me, she was already 41 years old, quite old for a Cambodian mother. She had thought she would not have any more children, that the health risks were too great. Besides, a new child would be another burden on an already large family. So, she almost had an abortion, but my eldest sister convinced her to go through with the pregnancy. My sister warned that Cambodia's medical facilities weren't very good, and that an abortion would be much more dangerous than carrying me to term. And so she did.

My mother never told me any of this as a child. I learned it from my older sister when I was grown up. It is strange to know that I came so close to not being born. It makes me reflect. For a lot of my life, I have been unlucky, though for some of it I have been very lucky indeed. It makes a certain kind of sense that my luck started so early on in life— lucky to have been able to start life in the first place!

My family was not so rich, so my brothers and sisters either helped at home or worked to earn money. My second older sister, Heang, prepared rice porridge for the entire family, and my brother, Heng, worked as a street vendor selling bread and sandwiches. My oldest brother, Nguon, was a mechanic who fixed bicycles and motorcycles. Because I was the youngest, I stayed mostly at home or played with other children my age around the neighborhood. I have many memories of my older siblings, especially my sister Heang, because they were usually the ones who looked after me. My mother was often too busy to supervise me herself, and in Cambodia, older siblings help out by parenting the younger ones.

They would take me down to a nearby river to bathe. We used ash, sand or coconut bark fibers to brush our teeth. We had no toilet, so we dug a hole in the ground, did our business, and buried it. Older children and adults used a leaf to wipe themselves when they were done, but young children would have to call an older sibling or parent to help them. A brother or sister would pour water down the child's backside.

My siblings went to primary school, but only the oldest ones were given the option of pursuing education beyond that. I was too young for school. Instead, I played and sometimes helped with light chores. Sometimes Ma would ask me to massage her tired and tense muscles. I have memories of her asking me to pull the white hairs from her head.

My sister Heang has told me that my brother Chhay, the second-youngest child, and I were our mother's favorites. Perhaps it was because we were the youngest, and so she was most protective of us. My older siblings remember that they couldn't tease me, because I would cry easily and then my mother would scold or punish them. Crying, it seems, was an effective weapon to stop them, and that's how I used it—not as a form of weakness, but as a way to fight back against them.

#

I spent most of my time playing outside with other children, barefoot and fearless. That's the way it was, and largely still is, in Cambodia. Almost from the time they first walk, children have freedom to go off by themselves, without an adult watching over them. They learn to climb trees, to swim, to run. Relying on themselves this way builds great self-confidence.

We had lots of games. Sometimes, we picked flamboyant flowers that were still young and inside their buds and asked our playmates to guess—would the flower inside still be white or already red? We played with whatever simple things we could find. Once we made dinnerware from river clay.

One of my happiest childhood activities is this: under the silver kiss of full moonlight, going out with other children at night to catch crickets. Carrying water in a small plastic scoop, we scanned the ground for crickets' homes, small holes in the ground. When we found one, we poured in water and waited crouching, ready to catch the occupants when they came out of the hole. It was a lot of fun to collect the crickets, which mother would fry. As they are for many Cambodians, fried crickets were our favorite snack. They smelled like roasted peanuts, very crunchy and tasty especially females full of eggs.

We would keep one or two crickets in a matchbox, to use as musical pets. To keep mine happy, I put in a leaf for food and made small holes in the matchbox to let them breathe. To make them sing, we pulled out one of our hairs, folded the strand into two or three, then used it to tickle the cricket's bottom. That would make it rub its forewings together and create a cheerful chirping music. We competed among ourselves to see who would make the cricket sing loudest.

But as with all children, our games could be cruel. We sometimes played with green mint leaf beetles and the leaves of the tree known as the flamboyant. We stripped all the leaves off a stem except for the last few. Then, we pushed the stem into the anus of the bug before launching it in the air, and laughed, following the poor thing until we couldn't see the fluttering leaves anymore.

Sometimes wildlife got its revenge. One day we were playing in the backyard between the banana trees. I suddenly felt a strange sensation inside my bottom; something was wiggling there. I put my hand in my panties to pull it out. It was a huge, round, white Ascaris worm. I screamed. My sister Heang came to my rescue—she killed the thing with a sharp shovel, and buried it in the garden. I was petrified, disgusted and horrified that this beast had come out of my body!

I don't know if this was the cause, but even now I fear any creepy-crawly thing without legs, from earthworms to snakes to slugs.

I had trouble with larger animals, too.

One day, I was on a reddish dirt road, a mother hen was walking there with her chicks, scratching and pecking here and there, teaching them to find food. The little chicks were cute, little balls of yellow and grey moving at a jerky pace. I was walking through the flock, and some of the chicks started to squeak in alarm, unable to see their mother past my legs. Suddenly, she took action! She jumped up at my face, completely obscuring my vision with her beating wings, scratching at me with her claws! I was so terrified that all I could do was scream and burst into tears. She scratched my lip with her claw, and I panicked even more as my tears mingled with my blood and red liquid fell to the ground!

My sister had to pick up a long stick of wood to fight off the hen, which ran away with her babies. The hen was so evil, my sister declared, that she had wanted to kill her and make a delicious chicken soup! According to her, I had a fear of chickens and chicks for a long time afterwards. And even now, I still have a small scar on my lip.

Sometimes, my friends and I played doctors and patients. Perhaps this was a glimpse of the career I had ahead of me, as I was always the doctor, giving injections in the buttocks of my friends, using a twig as a needle. Being a doctor was a highly respected role in Cambodian society. Perhaps, even as a small child, I was ambitious. I was certainly inquisitive and adventurous. I was often the one to suggest the games that we played, a sort of gentle leader to my playmates.

During the rainy season, flood waters sometimes closed in. Like most houses in rural Cambodia, ours was built on stilts, so we were high and dry, but the water could get so deep that we couldn't get out to play. When this happened, I tried to catch fish through a hole in our bamboo-strip floor. I attached a hook to some sewing thread with a grain of cooked rice on the end of the hook. Sometimes, the rice fell off in the water, but I never got discouraged. I tried again and patiently waited for a fish to bite. I don't recall catching any, though. The fish were certainly smart enough to take the free food and swim away.

#

Our culture taught us to be respectful of our elders. In my case, the most respected members of my family were my grandparents. I wanted to show my respect and love for my grandmother, so as a child, I sometimes saved some small dried fish to give to her. Of course, one's pockets—especially the pockets of a child who plays outdoors in the dirt every day—are not the best place to keep food of any sort, but a child doesn't think of that sort of thing. Also, an adult might not see dried fish as the best gift, but I didn't think of that, either because it was one of my favorite foods. I don't recall where I got the fish from, I just remember that I was excited to give my grandmother such a nice gift.

Children in Cambodia were expected to obey their elders, and paid a price, sometimes a harsh one, if they didn't. Because there were so many children in our household, parents didn't have time to explain the punishment they doled out, and children weren't able to ask what they'd done to deserve it. I recall my father punishing one of my brothers by hanging him upside down with a rope in the middle of the house. I don't remember what the infraction was, but I also don't remember being angry with my father about it. We all respected our parents, even when they punished us harshly.

One time in the kitchen, my mother got angry at my sister Heang, so she took a wooden log from the pile for the fire, and hit Heang on the head with it. When I saw her head bleeding, I was scared

14

and I rushed to Heang to try to save her. Again, I don't know why she was punished. I only remember being scared for her—and for myself. The memory of that moment remains very vivid to me. I was compassionate over my sister's pain, my fear for her life, and panic at the scene. It left a lasting impact.

As a child, I had no idea of how life worked. I had never seen a birth, or a death. I believed life was a cycle: a baby became a child, a child became an adult, and then an adult became a baby again, without dying. Whenever I was punished for something, I would tell myself that when I became an adult, and my mother and elder siblings were children again, I would ensure that they got their just rewards in return! I would often tell myself this, out loud, when I faced injustices. Quietly talking to myself, in fact, became a coping mechanism that I would employ at later difficult times in my life.

Looking back now, I can almost understand my parents' actions. They were doing their best to keep us safe and alive without much money or time. In any case, I don't want to over-emphasize these punishments. Actually, I feel quite content with my childhood, and I remember the freedom of my early childhood fondly. Overall, I recall it as a time of happiness and innocence, before and just after the Khmer Rouge.

-2-
A Childhood Stolen: The Khmer Rouge Years

I was born in 1970, the same year the war began. But for a long time, I wasn't aware of it. I was a small child, concerned with plucking my mother's gray hairs and catching crickets, and in any case the fighting had remained far away from our home in Kampong Phnom. But by 1973, it was drawing near, and so most of my family moved to Phnom Penh, the capital. Only my father and my brother stayed behind, to watch over the house.

At the time, the capital was under the control of Lon Nol. He was a general and the prime minister. In 1970, he had overthrown the country's long-time leader, Norodom Sihanouk, and that event touched off the war. My parents thought we would be safe in Phnom Penh. There had been talk of going to Vietnam, which to some people seemed a safer place, despite its own war. But Pa didn't want us to go. He believed Cambodia's conflict would resolve itself soon, and we could go home.

We spent the next two years living in Phnom Penh in a rented house. The city was growing swollen with refugees like us, people seeking haven from the war. Rockets were hitting the city. But at times life could seem normal. Certainly it did to me—I have very few memories from this time, good or bad.

One of the good ones is that some mornings when I woke up, I would find that my brother Heng, the street vendor, had put a French baguette in my hand. If he did not sell all the bread from his stall, he brought some back for me. The first thing I saw when I opened my eyes was the golden, crunchy crust, which made me wonder whether it was real or I was still dreaming.

Of course, Pa had been wrong about the war ending quickly. The Khmer Rouge continued to fight Lon Nol's army, and on April 17, 1975, they entered Phnom Penh. Many people lined the streets to cheer their arrival, thinking that a period of peace and reconciliation would begin. But instead the Khmer Rouge issued orders that everyone had to leave the city, immediately.

My real memories of the war begin here. I and my family joined the exodus—hundreds of thousands of people marching into the countryside. Most had no idea where they were going, but we did. We would head for our old house fifty kilometers away. I remember being frightened by the noise and chaos around me, and holding Heang's hand as we walked, loaded with basic belongings like clothes and mosquito nets. From time to time, she pulled my hand to walk faster or dragged me when I stopped. We were surrounded by countless other people on dirt roads, fleeing just like us.

At one point we walked past an old woman. She lifted her sarong; we could see her private parts hanging down. She asked for help, but we hurried on, in part to avoid the indecent sight. We just had to keep walking to escape and get back home. Now, looking back, I wonder if she was suffering from a prolapse. As a child, of course, I didn't think in medical terms like that. I was only shocked to see such a thing in public.

We walked for days. Exhaustion set in. At night I didn't care that I had to sleep on the road under a mosquito net. I didn't care that I might be hit by a passing truck. I just wanted to rest after a full day of walking in the heat.

When we neared our village, my brother Nguon ran ahead to find Father and let him know we were coming back. What a relief it was when we spotted him walking against the torrent of people to get to us and help us carry everything.

We thought we had reached safety. We moved back into our old house and hoped that the old life would resume. For a brief period, it did. But a family living together in its own house did not fit into Khmer Rouge notions of creating a new Cambodia. Everyone, they decreed, would be loyal to angkar, as their all-powerful governing apparatus was known—"the organization." That required the breaking of family loyalties. So families were split up into separate camps. Men went into one camp, women into another. All children, the Khmer Rouge deemed, were children of angkar and their natural parents would not take care of them. They would go into age-based children's camps. Though for a while I escaped that fate, remaining with my mother, I was soon moved to a camp of a type known as mondol koma (children's center) for children aged three to five.

My recollections of this place, located not far from our house, are sparse. Perhaps, torn away from my family, I subconsciously suppressed memories of what happened there. Somehow, though, I coped. One thing I do recall is that, though the Khmer Rouge generally abolished education, in this camp they gave us a little bit of schooling—the alphabet and numbers and not much else. We took lessons outside in the shade of a tree, using lumps of coal to write on a square of areca palm leaf cover (it's known technically as a leaf sheath) functioning as a slate board. Only just recently, I met a distant relative who told me she remembered me being in this camp with her. I was nice to her, she said, and helped her give the teacher correct answers.

After a year or so, I was put into a camp for children roughly aged six to eight, though it was more according to physical size than age. There was no teaching here, and we were told we were now too old to eat and sleep for free. We would have to work. But because we were still very young, we were given simple tasks, such as chasing birds away from planted rice fields. I can't say it was hard—sometimes to my childish imagination it seemed like a game. But just about everything else in this camp was an ordeal.

At night, we were packed into a sleeping shelter like sardines, lying head to foot to head. The floor was uneven, and sometimes children wet themselves at night. Their urine flowed along the floor, often past my head. In the morning, we woke up wet and smelly. There were lice as well. We were always itchy from them.

But most of all, we were starving.

The Khmer Rouge fed us morning glory (also called water spinach), a vegetable that was normally slop for pigs. It was cut coarsely and cooked in water in a huge pot with a small amount of rice. The soup was thin and bland, and smelled like morning glory sap, which usually turned it black or brown. From that one pot the entire camp was served. One memory I have is from the times we awaited our food. I always hoped that a small, white river fish had been accidentally caught up in the morning glory and that I might get it in my bowl. Sometimes I did get one, but it was extremely rare. I was enduring long periods without vital nutrients. Severe malnutrition was setting in. I was too young to notice, but other people could see that my abdomen was bloating, a classic sign of too little food.

During the day, as we went around on our duties, we snatched up any food we could find. This was the first time I ever ate raw green tomatoes. I still recall their smell, their warmth from the sun, picked fresh from the plant. They were hairy, but juicy, and I savored them. I also dug up and ate my old favorites, sweet potatoes, when I could.

The Khmer Rouge are remembered for brutal regimentation, and we saw plenty of that. But at times they could be careless and disorganized in keeping tabs on people. This allowed other members of the family to see me from time to time and bring me food.

Ma had somehow managed to remain living at the family house, though she had to go out daily to work the communal rice fields. But she was too terrified of angkar to steal food. I think she preferred to risk dying of starvation rather than getting discovered by them.

Food smuggling fell to my sister Heang and brother Heng. In doing this, they were risking their lives—if they'd been found out, they would probably have been executed. This special supply was by no means regular—my siblings were not always nearby. Each had been placed in another of the Khmer Rouge's heartless institutions of social regimentation, the "mobile unit." These were groups of children who were moved from place to place to carry out whatever hard labor was required—the digging of canals, the clearing of forest, the preparation of fields for rice planting. This kept Heang and Heng away from our area for extended periods, but when they came back they made heroic efforts to contact us. Heang in particular was cunning enough to move around, sneaking when that made sense, pleading with Khmer Rouge leaders for permission when that was the better approach.

One of Heang's tactics was to ask to be in a work group that went out in the morning to cut bamboo. During the labor, she would sneak away to the other camps to bring us food. I had to eat it without being noticed, stuffing my mouth quickly and discreetly with my back turned to everyone, so nobody saw. If I was caught, Heang would be too. Sometimes she brought me a single big rice ball with a shrimp hidden inside. What a delicacy it was to me! The jasmine smell of the white rice, the sweetness, the sticky texture. I don't recall ever eating rice so delicious since then. But Heang also collected animals she could find in the wild, like rats and frogs, which she roasted and brought to me. Sometimes I wanted to save some of the food in my pocket for later. But my sister said no. She would wait with me to make sure I finished. She was afraid that if I didn't eat everything right away, I'd be caught with it or the other children would steal it from me.

I have one clear memory of my father from the Khmer Rouge time, and he gave me food too. It's my only clear memory of him at all, in fact. One day, I think just before he was sent to a men's camp, he lifted me onto his shoulders and we walked to his work site, a collection of pits that people were digging. I enjoyed the swaying view that I got as he walked. For me, it was a new perspective from Pa's height. Suddenly I felt privileged not only just to have Pa for myself but that he was carrying me. That made me feel loved. He gave the lunch box that I carried in one hand while the other held his head. The single sweet potato inside the box was a treasure for me. I am quite sure that he had denied it to himself so that his little girl might have something special and nourishing.

It's entirely possible that I owe my life today to these gifts of food. Without them, I might have ended up as one of the millions of people who succumbed in those years to starvation and easily treatable disease.

I don't mean to suggest that visits from family were common. More typically I was alone, or with other children. One day, after a rainfall, I was with one of the other girls in a ditch that passed some distance from the camp. I called her "comrade," a political term that the Khmer Rouge insisted we use. We were bathing in the water, washing away our bodies' build-up of dirt and urine. We felt so good at becoming clean that we didn't notice that the rest of our group had left us behind. We didn't know how to get back to the camp, so instead we tried to find our way to our old homes. We were afraid we'd be punished for not fulfilling our duties, so we carried loads of hay on our heads, even in the darkness, lost and exhausted, to show our Khmer Rouge masters that, even when lost, we were not forgetting our duty.

As we crossed a small, broken wooden bridge in the dark, I fell into the river below. I was trapped, entangled in water plants, mostly big hyacinths above my head on the water's surface. I panicked, kicking and fighting against the plants. I screamed for my friend to go and get my mother to help, but I scared her so badly that she ran to her own house and left me behind.

Finally, exhausted and unable to keep resisting, I surrendered. I was ready to die. But then my feet touched the muddy bottom of the river. I realized that the water was actually quite shallow. I jumped up and down on my toes, fighting for breath, until I reached the river's bank. I was exhausted, relieved to be alive, but at the same time embarrassed and ashamed. Completely muddy and soaked, I was able to reach home and find my mother.

Later on as a young adult, I often dreamed that I was being chased by someone who terrified me. No matter how much I tried to run fast, I could barely move forward. It was like trying to run through water. I always woke up before I was caught, out of breath, sweating, my heart pounding. I feel that this dream was born from that terrifying fall in the water.

Though I coped, I never got used to being in this unnatural situation. At times I grew extremely homesick. Once I deliberately escaped from the children's camp. I remember crawling under surveillance light beams and somehow finding my way back home. Heang was there too, and the next morning, Ma asked her to take me back to the camp. The only food she ever got was her ration from angkar, so she didn't have enough to feed me. At the children's camp, I would at least get a little food, she said. My mother was also scared that angkar would notice that I was gone. I wasn't the only one who would be punished. My whole family could face retribution.

When my sister brought me back, she had to explain to the camp leaders why I had left. She begged them to forgive me. Thankfully, she finally convinced them, and I was only made to swear not to do it again.

Later I again began missing home terribly. Heang took pity on me— she recalls that I was skinny, chronically ill and dirty and with a horrible bloated abdomen. She successfully begged the camp leaders to let her take me home for a day, even though it was already late in the evening. The rainy season was unusually heavy that year, and everything was flooded. The roads and stilt houses were inundated, and Heang carried me home on her back. We had to cross a water channel. The water got deeper and deeper, so she put me on her shoulders while she tried to swim. I grew more and more afraid we were going to perish drowned. When we were only partway across, I clutched her neck and head so tightly that, without realizing it, I almost drowned us both. While she struggled to loosen my grip, I fell off and was dragged away by the current. She screamed my name, got no response, and thought I might have drowned. She was terribly frightened about how she would explain it to our mother. She felt so relieved when, at the house, she found me hugging one of its stilts.

Perhaps this means I have always been a survivor, willing to fight to get through hard times. The memory of that episode is still vivid for my sister, although I myself have forgotten it. It's possible, though, that this event caused me to fear deep water later in life. Now, whenever I am in it, especially when I can't see the bottom, I feel an empty hole in my stomach start to grow.

-3-
Rescue

We could not imagine this life ever ending, then suddenly it did. In late 1978, the army of Vietnam, accompanied by Cambodian liberators, entered our country to overthrow the Khmer Rouge. It so happened that our camps were right in the invasion path. With the army approaching, the Khmer Rouge stopped all work and began ordering us to flee into the forest with them. Of course no one wanted to go—we saw freedom near, and wondered too what angkar would do to us in the forest. Early on the morning of January 7, 1979, the liberation force reached right to our camps. Cambodian soldiers with the Vietnamese shouted to us loudly to take cover. Somehow we managed not to be taken off by the Khmer Rouge, but in the course of it we got a brief and terrifying exposure to war. Suddenly gunshots were sounding, and we were all bending over and running as fast as we could, dropping what we were carrying, trying to find a hole or whatever we could to protect us. I saw small flying lights in the sky. Loud explosions shook the ground, suspending dust in the air. "BOOM!" "BOOSH!" "BAM!" I think there was the sound of helicopters too, and military trucks. All of it created hysterical screaming that was wildly contagious—many people joined in, shouting at the top of their voices.

But then it was over. The Khmer Rouge had fled. The Vietnamese and Cambodian liberators immediately continued their advance toward the capital Phnom Penh. They entered the city at noon that same day and proclaimed an end to the Khmer Rouge government.

#

Here's another memory. I am on the back of a water buffalo in the rice fields and muddy puddles which are dotted with colorful lotus flowers and purple water hyacinths. I sink gently into the muddy water with the buffalo when he takes a bath.

Heang says this was after the Khmer Rouge. We all had to fend for ourselves in this period. People seized whatever they could, some of it things the Khmer Rouge had left behind. My brother Nguon was able to catch a large, skeletal ox, which our family traded for a pair of water buffalos.

There was no school to attend, so my brother Chhay and I took care of the buffalos, bringing them to graze in the fields, and lazing on their backs. That was, and is today, a common sight in the Cambodian countryside—a small child dozing atop one of these huge gentle animals.

It was 1979 or 80 now. We had returned to the old house. Like before, we lived close to nature. I remember walking under the moonlight to the river behind our house to bathe. If I needed to relieve myself, I crouched on the end of the half-broken wooden floating dock and did my business in the water, then turned to watch as a swarm of small fish rushed to eat the poo. It was always amazing to me when I think that I had spent years hoping for just one to turn up in my bowl of water spinach soup—these would be food for us one day, and yet here they were, eating my poo.

Indeed, thought about food was constant, driven by our memories of what starvation felt like. When storms came, I and other children ran through the wind and rain toward huge mango trees. When the wind knocked fruit down, we raced to pick it up, though the first falls were always overripe, rotten or bad. When good ones did fall, they hit the ground with enough force to burst them, but I was still happy and proud to bring them home and share them with my family.

Other times, I walked in the hot sun through fallow sweet potato fields that lay near our house, looking for small green shoots—the lone potatoes that had been missed in the early harvests. Every time I spotted one in the hard, dry ground, I rushed to it, heart pounding. I dug into the dirt with my bare hands, as fast as I could, but carefully. I didn't want to break the sweet potato underneath. I always hoped for a large one.

Often I was disappointed, but that never stopped or discouraged me. I kept scanning the fields for these hidden treasures.

We caught live fish, and we looked for dead ones too, floating down the Mekong. Upstream from us, encamped Vietnamese soldiers sometimes fished by setting off grenades in the water. Currents assured that the soldiers didn't gather them all. Sometimes my family members risked drowning to swim far out from the bank and collect floating fish. Bringing in a big one was cause for celebration. It became a fermented fish dish and fed the whole family for days.

We were without Pa now. I only found out at this time what had happened to him. He was killed around the end of 1977. He had been assigned to an adult men's camp in another village with one of his brothers. One day, there was to be a mass political rally bringing together people from all over the commune, which included three other villages where the rest of our family members had been assigned. It was going to be an opportunity for us all to see each other, at least from a distance, but we might have a few brief moments together. Members of our family arrived. But not Pa.

First came a commemoration of the Chinese leader Mao Tse-tung, who had died the year before. There were lots of political speeches. But then came a terrible message from one of our cousins. He told our family that the Khmer Rouge had declared that my father, the cousin's father and other men hosted in their bodies an "enemy spirit," which meant they were not pure, not fervent for the Khmer Rouge regime. That spirit, the local Khmer Rouge said, must be rooted out. My sister Heang says we all had to hold our sorrow and not show any feelings. Otherwise they would kill us too as a fraternity of the impure. It seems he had not come to the rally because he and my uncle had already been taken away for "education." The Khmer Rouge used often euphemisms. In this case, education meant being killed. Indeed, we never saw father or my uncle again.

Soon after that, all members of our uncle's family were executed for this same reason. Somehow, almost all of my own family members were spared. But we did lose one brother, named Kuong, of whom I have only a vague memory. Kuong was the one who had stayed with Pa to look after our house in the village when the rest of us moved to Phnom Penh.

#

During this period I became close to a young woman named Sophy, wife of my brother Nguon. The story behind their marriage was quite unusual. During the Khmer Rouge time, Nguon had been ordered to marry another woman, a stranger. Forced marriage was a common tool of angkar social engineering. But Nguon already knew Sophy, a distant relative, and so strong was the attraction that he decided to contest the marriage order. You'll recall that Nguon had been a bicycle and motorcycle mechanic before the Khmer Rouge victory. He had continued that work under the new order. Perhaps it was because he had proved valuable in this work that the Khmer Rouge relented on the question of marriage. Nguon and Sophy were united as husband and wife.

After the angkar's overthrow, I went swimming in the brown Mekong one day with the two of them and Heang. In fact I didn't yet know how to swim properly, so I was hugging a banana trunk like a buoy (I think my old fear of drowning had kicked in). Heang and I began to quarrel over who would have the trunk. I was cursing, even at that young age, and Nguon thought I was addressing his wife, so he became angry with me. He shoved me, and the banana trunk slipped from my arms. I bobbed like a yo-yo in the current, fighting for breath and swallowing brown river water. It was Sophy who saved me from drowning by grabbing my long hair and pulling me out of danger. My brother was still mad at me and ordered me to get out of the river.

We went back to the house. I was angry, scared and shocked, crying all the way back. When we got there, my brother told my mother his version of the story and she punished me once again. She whipped me with a long, thin tree branch with the leaves stripped from it. I cried even harder and louder, full of anger at the injustice! Ma had not even given me a chance to explain.

I thought it was so unfair that the next day, gathering with my little friends, I performed some black magic. I lit a candle, covered it with a coconut shell, and wished a goiter on my mother. With a wooden stick, I knocked three times on the coconut shell. I don't remember where I learned the spell, but thankfully it didn't work!

#

At some time after the fall of the Khmer Rouge, Nguon and Sophy fled with Sophy's family, the Iengs, to Vietnam. There, they filled out application documents to go to France as political refugees. They had good hope of success: Sophy's brother Richard had moved to France before the Khmer Rouge victory of 1975. Now he was petitioning to bring the rest of his family there.

One day, Sophy came back to our house for a visit. She brought me presents: a nice yellow tutu dress, wooden shoes and a satchel. I was enchanted! They were the best gifts I could ever have wished for.

Sophy has told me that during that visit I told her I had had nightmares about the Khmer Rouge torturing me (today I don't remember such dreams, however). But we all did fear they were going to come back. I begged Sophy to take me to Vietnam. She insisted that I should tell my mother myself that I wanted to go.

I did, but it was mainly Sophy who made arguments to help convince her, such as that I was the youngest of the family, and I would more easily adapt to a new country, that I would learn a new language faster because of my age. Then, once I found success in the new country, I could help my family back in Cambodia, as Sophy's brother had, and maybe even bring everyone to France.

Ma finally agreed, and she gave me many instructions: I had to listen, obey, work hard, and study well and never be a burden to whomever would care for me in the new place. My family members asked me over and over if I was sure I wanted to go, but I was certain. I said yes, I was happy to go. I didn't cry, though the rest of my family did.

Perhaps the Khmer Rouge camp had already taught me to be determined, strong, and independent, hiding my tears and my fears from other people, because I had plenty of apprehensions.

We travelled first to the capital, Saigon, in a big, packed truck. I was just tall enough to poke my head over the side of the truck. On the road beneath us, vendors sold salty dried shells and fruits. The food looked delicious, and so colorful —I wanted to eat it all!

Eventually we arrived at a refugee camp in Song Be, outside Saigon.

#

We settled in for a long wait while officials processed our papers. Nguon, Sophy, and the Ieng family had already submitted theirs and could not add me to their family list without having to reprocess everything, which would delay their departure for France. Instead, they added me to the family of relatives who were at the camp, the Pou family. They gave me a new name on the documents, and, for some reason, a 1972 birthday. The war and Khmer Rouge years upended basic things like birthdates, but I've been assured that I was in fact born in late 1970.

We didn't know which family would reach France first, but we planned that if the Pou family went first, I would stay with Sophy's brother, Richard Ieng, who was already in France, until Nguon and Sophy arrived.

In the camp in Vietnam, I followed Sophy around most of the time like she was a second mother. She took good care of me and I liked her as much as my mother and sister Heang. She took me for haircuts and manicures, and all sorts of "girly" treats. She didn't have children of her own then, so I think she thought of me as her own child. She told me recently that I was a nice, obedient, easy-going, and honest.

I played jump rope with other children and went hunting for mushrooms and vegetables. We cultivated vegetables, such as winged beans. The beans grew on poles and over trellises, and as children, we were small enough to sneak under the trellises and look for beans to eat. Sometimes, small green snakes would hang camouflaged among the trellises. It would always scare me to death to touch one and realize it wasn't actually a long, delicious bean! But it was always worth the risk.

One day, Miss You, one of Sophy's sisters, went to take a shower in the small bathing hut that was built with palm leaves and twigs. Suddenly, we heard a loud scream from the hut and everyone rushed to rescue her. There was a python in the shower with her! The men caught it, and the next day, we made a delicious soup out of it with pickled lime. (This was not, by the way, because we were short of food. Eating snake meat is not uncommon in Cambodia.)

After life under the Khmer Rouge, it was of course a great privilege to have plenty to eat. In fact, one of my very best memories of childhood food comes from my time at the Song Be camp.

In the early morning one day, Sophy's mother (she was my great-aunt) called me and Sophy's youngest sister Tieng to accompany her to the market. I think that a few days earlier, Sophy's mother had received some money from her son in France. Now we were going to have a good time.

Walking and holding her hand, I felt my heart start to pound with the intuition that she would treat us to a delicious breakfast soup. Kuyteav is made with fine rice noodles in simmered pork bone broth. Nowadays, it's called Phnom Penh soup, and is similar to Vietnamese pho. The white bowl would contain fresh, crisp bean sprouts and chewy noodles in the broth, topped off with ground pork and a few slices of boiled liver. You could customize the flavor with fried garlic, pepper, soy sauce, fish sauce, lime, preserved radish, chopped coriander, and pickled green chili peppers.

I left the bowl clean. I sucked the bones from the soup broth until all the marrow was gone. I chewed the soft parts of the bone, and nibbled every last piece of cartilage off them.

If I close my eyes, I can feel myself sitting on a wooden stool in the busy, muddy aisles of the local market. I can feel my mouth watering at the smell, waiting impatiently as the vendors filled the bowl with kuyteav soup and perfumed condiments. I can feel a glowing sense of well-being.

If only all my experiences in the camp were good ones. I was the youngest child in both the Ieng and Pou families, and the other young adults liked to tease me until I got upset and cried. Sometimes they would hang me upside down, though I begged them to stop. My cousin Tieng sometimes pinched me just to make me cry, because she did not like to see me around her mother. Once, the youngest Pou boy chased me, trying to put my own wet, washed panties on my head. There is a superstition in Cambodia that if you wear panties on your head, you will become ignorant and be unable to learn. I tried to outrun him, terrified about my future intelligence, but he was too fast. I was so angry and frustrated! I missed the protection of my own family during these times. I often felt alone without anyone to defend or understand me.

I also envied my cousins, because they had such close relationships with their mother and sisters. I remember one night under the moon and stars, my older aunt from the Pou family, who we called Mamie, told us moral tales and myths. I loved those sorts of stories. My imagination would run enchanted and free. Even when I got older, I loved stories and movies like this, with a strong moral sense, stories that encourage gratitude, honesty, justice, dignity, bravery, and honor.

One day we left the camp to visit Saigon—now called Ho Chi Minh City—and I got to see a play in a theatre. I didn't understand most of it, because the actors sang in Vietnamese or Chinese. Nevertheless, it was like magic for me. One of my relatives leaned over and explained what was happening. The story was fairly easy to follow. The whole evening is one of my most precious memories—a wonderful play, vibrant costumes and magical story, and being in a lively, brightly lit city.

Another time, a young couple in the Pou (Miss. Pol and Mr. Na) family got permission to go for a walk in Saigon. Sophy had me go with them. Because I was young and naïve, she was using me to spy on the couple's relationship. However, she recounted to me later that when she asked me what they'd done that day, all I could say was that I ate ice-cream and fruit, rode in a cyclo (a cycle rickshaw) and saw another play.

In the refugee camp, I got my first taste of real education. Before going to my new country, I had to learn some basic French sentences and vocabulary. This was the first time I had a proper school book. It was called *"Méthode Boscher ou La Journée des Tout Petits"* ("The Boscher Method or the Young Children's Day"). The cover was brightly-colored, and showed two blond children, Daniel and Valérie, sitting and reading under a red apple tree, surrounded by beautiful flowers. I was thrilled to own it, and took very good care of it.

Cambodia follows the Buddhist calendar, and usually New Year's celebrations are in April. The chicken is an important part of the celebration, and our relatives wanted to prepare a rooster for the ceremony. My brother Nguon was the one who slaughtered the rooster. He nominated me to be his assistant, instructing me in the process. Following the Buddhist tradition, we asked for forgiveness as we prepared to kill the bird. I prayed it would be more fortunate in its next life and not be reincarnated as another animal. I didn't like to think that it would have to be killed for food again.

I held the chicken's feet while Nguon held the wings. He tucked its head back between its wings and plucked part of the neck to expose its skin, then cut its throat with a long, sharp knife. We bled it first by holding it upside down, collecting the blood in a bowl with a bit of salt. I was terrified! I turned away, and tried not to watch.

The rooster was kicking so hard that my whole body jerked as I tried to hold it. Nguon was mad at my squeamishness and scolded me. I kept telling myself that this would be over very soon, but it seemed to take forever to empty the rooster's blood and hear my brother tell me I could let the chicken go.

And my ordeal wasn't over! Once I let the chicken go, despite its slit throat, it flapped its wings and came running at me! Again, I was on the receiving end of an angry chicken.

#

As it turned out, good luck settled on the Pou family and me. After only eight months, a short wait in the world of refugees, we learned we would go to France. Sophy and Nguon's documents still weren't approved, so we would leave without them. Soon we rode out of the camp, headed to the Saigon airport. It was a bright sunny day under the heat. At the airport, we walked slowly, one step at a time, along hot asphalt, me holding a Pou family member's hand. On our right, a long diamond-meshed security fence held back a crowd. I saw many emotional faces behind that fence but no familiar ones. People seemed hysterical, waving, calling, yelling, and crying all at the same time. Some were looking for family members.

Suddenly I saw in front of me a giant white airplane, a Boeing airbus. I was in awe. It was my first sight of an airplane close-up. I was feeling sorrow over separation from my loved ones. But mostly I was feeling excitement about boarding this thing and flying off to live in a new country. We had heard so many good things about France. It seemed like the Promised Land; we were awaiting a paradise in a bright future!

I was 10 years old. It was August 1981.

—Part Two—
France

-4-
Becoming a French Girl

After long hours on the plane, we arrived in France. There we were taken to the refugee center in Creteil, a southeastern suburb of Paris. New arrivals went there to be medically screened before going on to their new homes. My official records show that I stood 1.3 meters tall (4 feet, 3 inches) and weighed 22 kilograms (49 pounds). I can't begin to guess how much heavier I was than during the starvation years of Khmer Rouge rule.

I remember the smell of fresh bread and coffee from the canteen at the refugee center. That was the first time I'd ever smelled *café au lait*.

We stayed there perhaps two weeks and then joined other members of the Pou family in a suburb of Paris. But from there we dispersed. The Pou children stayed with their parents, but I was told that we would stick with the plan that Richard Ieng would take me until my brother Nguon came to get me.

I went to join Richard but it turned out he couldn't look after me. He was busy with his job as a waiter in a brewery, working night shifts. So after a few days I was given to another uncle, Sophon, who owned a Chinese restaurant. That didn't work either, and finally I was sent to the Red Cross orphanage in Issy-les-Molineaux, south of Paris. It was a center specifically for Southeast Asian orphan refugees.

I had arrived in this country with lots of family support, but somehow I had now become an orphan. I would stay at the Red Cross facility until a French family could take me for foster care. At that point, I would lose contact with the Pou family and my uncles Richard and Sophon, and therefore with the rest of my natural family—and they with me. I would become invisible to them.

Later I learned that my mother had been very angry with Sophy and Nguon for letting me leave for France and losing contact with me. In the years that followed, when Heang had children of her own, Ma was always telling them about me so that they'd have some concept of me even though we'd never met. Ma often laid back in her hammock, her arm resting on her forehead, and, it seems, her mind on me. She kept her memories of me alive and vibrant for years. She wondered where her youngest child was at that instant. She worried I would be unable to eat French food. Certainly after the Khmer Rouge regime, food was one of the most important concerns in Cambodian life. People had lived with miniscule rations for so long that they remained forever worried about that essential aspect of survival.

But on the other side of the world, I was doing all I could to forget my past. I just wanted to become a French girl and lead a normal French life.

#

I stayed at the Issy-les-Moulineaux orphanage for about two months. You're not supposed to have such memories about an orphanage, but I have fond ones of the place.

It was full of Asian children: some Vietnamese and Laotian but many others Cambodian like me. Maybe it was because I was the youngest there, or because the others saw me as a lovely girl, but I felt loved and protected all the time I was there. My older "sisters" and "brothers" were always at my side. I held their hands whenever we went somewhere and crossed streets. I don't recall missing my real family at all.

We were given second-hand clothes and shoes, and every week we got a small allowance to spend on ourselves. For the first time, I ate green apples—we bought them because we liked the sour taste. Cambodians like to eat fruit when it is still green, with condiments made of sugar, salt, and chili. Many of the children, especially the older teenagers, had trouble adjusting to French food. When they got sick of what was available in the orphanage canteen, they ate Asian instant noodles and boiled eggs in the dormitory rooms.

One thing I didn't like about the orphanage was that every Wednesday, some of us had dentist appointments. Perhaps my teeth were among the worst, because I had to go over and over.

Each time it felt like a torture session. Lying on the chair, trying to keep my mouth wide open and hold my breath, with the dazzling light over my face, and the whirring, spinning, whining sounds near my teeth!

When Wednesdays came and they called out names for the dentists, I always got very anxious. Then, one Wednesday, I was waiting, hoping I wouldn't be on the list—and I wasn't. The reason was that my French foster family was coming to pick me up.

It was the fifth time in three months that I had been moved to a different place, and with different people. I don't recall getting a chance to say goodbyes at the orphanage to my "brothers" and "sisters." They were all at their dentist appointments, or at other activities. I left with all my belongings in a small blue and white bag.

#

On November 5, 1981, at nearly eleven years old, I arrived at my new home in Roissy en Brie, which is about 35 kilometers from the center of Paris. My French mother had gone to some pains to try to make me feel welcome. On that first day family members and various neighbors presented gifts to me. The one I remember most was the first one: a lovely baby doll. I named him Tony. He came with a nursing bottle that could be filled with water, and after you fed him water, he would pee. They also gave me a bed sheet with "Nary" embroidered on it.

The gifts and the welcome by nice people enchanted and entertained me, but once everyone had gone home, and evening fell, it came to me that I was now to stay in this strange house permanently. I felt uncomfortable, lonely, and homesick for the orphanage, if such a thing is possible. I felt that everyone in the foster family was scrutinizing me. Up until then, I'd always been staying in places where there were plenty of Asian faces around. Here, there was nobody who looked like me. Even worse, I didn't know much French yet. I couldn't understand what my new mother was trying to say to me! The family members would all laugh or smile, and turn to look at me, and I would never know what was so funny. I felt like an animal in a zoo, being watched and talked about in words I couldn't understand.

My French mother—I came to call her maman, as most French children call their mothers—recalls that I ate very little that evening, and that I burst into tears at the table in front of my four foster siblings. I remember crying too when I went to bed that night, in the room I shared with my new sister, Christel.

In time, I settled down, and got to know them.

My foster father—I came to call him papa in the French way—was from a provincial middle-class family. As a young man, he served as a Paris firefighter, but by the time I joined the family, he had become an accountant. My foster mother was the daughter of a colonel in the Paris fire-fighting service. Her later-to-be husband had served under this colonel, and that's how they met. She had studied art, taught for a while at a vocational school, then moved to a nursery where she cared for small children. All in all, I would say, both my new parents had had comfortable childhoods, and received lots of love from their parents. Despite differences in education, they had the same basic values. One of these was strict adherence to the teachings of the Catholic church.

I had four foster siblings—three brothers and one sister. The eldest was Jean-François born in 1968, followed by my sister Christel in 1970, and the other two brothers, Ludovic born in 1971 and Eric born in 1972.

After I had grown up, maman told me that she had wanted to adopt a girl from Southeast Asia after seeing children in refugee camps on the news. She already had four children, of course, and due to her and my father's professions, they had modest means. In fact, they probably would have been turned down for adopting a refugee child, if she hadn't gotten advice from a friend who had adopted a Cambodian refugee. Inflate your wages on the application, she was told.

My French parents were on government assistance for large families while I was a child. We had just enough money to eat and go to school. My clothing was often second-hand from our cousins, or clothes that my older sister passed down to me when she grew out of them. Most of the clothes fit me, but sometimes they were too big. If I said they didn't fit, maman would say that I only had to grow a little more, and then they would be perfect. I later found out that papa had been unemployed for a few months while I was in school, and that was why they had put all of us kids into the canteen program at school, to ensure that we had at least one good, balanced meal every day.

But things like that made me wonder later on why they adopted me, since they had to lie about their income to get the application accepted. Regardless of taking pity on children seen on TV, why would maman choose to put even more financial stress on her family? I had not the courage to ask her. If I asked, it might seem that I am ungrateful, or that I resent her. That's not the case at all. I'm very grateful to her for taking me in, and for the opportunities that she gave me in France.

My new life, of course, involved more than adjusting to a new family. There was school. Considering my age, I should have been in grade 4 (CM1 in France), but because I didn't speak French, I was held back to grade 3 (CE2).

I had two teachers, Ms. Catherine and Ms. Roseline, who were very kind to me and sympathetic. They were always happy to help me when I was having trouble in class. They didn't scold me for not learning quickly, either. For homework, I had to do short exercises and readings. I could read by now, but I didn't understand most of the words. Nevertheless, I always tried to do all my homework well. I developed a system: First, I would work out what the question was, but if I could not understand it completely I would guess what they were trying to ask me. I would use context to try and work out all the unfamiliar words.

I spent a lot of time looking things up in the dictionary, but sometimes that only made me more confused. Some words had different meanings according to context, so instead of having just one new word to learn, I would have several.

To help me settle into the family, maman had taken a whole year off work, another sign of her commitment to me, but also another cause of financial stress. So on many days she helped me with my homework. So did Eric and Ludovic, the younger two of my brothers. For example, to help me memorize words for animals, they would mimic animal noises, playing around and jumping on the table to make me laugh. It was much easier to remember the words when I had these funny "lessons."

According to maman, I was smart, obedient, and a quick learner, but I could sometimes be stubborn. She also said that I was mature for my age, perhaps because of the things I had experienced back in Cambodia. (I would think that Ma's teachings to be a nice and obedient girl contributed too.) Homework always came first for me, before play, and I learned to sleep less in order to have more time to study. Under my blankets at night, with the lights off, I would still be reciting and memorizing my lessons from the day.

I was always afraid of letting people down, especially now my foster family, who I knew had done so much for me. I wanted to make them proud, to show them I was grateful that they had taken me in.

Nevertheless, there were days when no matter how hard I tried, I couldn't keep up. French is a very difficult language, with its complex verb forms, noun genders, and words pronounced differently depending on whether they are masculine or feminine. On the first day of school, we had to specify whether we would eat at school or at home. However, at the time, I didn't understand the word "canteen," so when most of the students in the class put their hands up to say yes about the canteen, I did as well, when I should have said no (it was later on that I did eat in the canteen, due to financial need).

Though my teachers were very supportive, some students mocked and teased me. I was the only Asian student at the school: other students who weren't white were of African or Arabic descent. At recess in the school playground, children from other classes sometimes pulled the corners of their eyes into a squint and called me *Chinetoque*, a slur for Chinese. They told racist jokes. They asked me why Chinese people had small eyes. Their answer: they were constipated, and their eyes got small because they had to push hard. They called me *bol de riz* (rice bowl), and mocked my haircut, which maman created herself with comb and scissors. They asked if I used a bowl to cut my fringe so straight. They often asked me why I had a French family, since I was Asian.

Sometimes they used words I didn't understand. When I got home, I asked maman what they meant, and she reacted with shock. She would not tell me the exact meaning only that the words were very ugly, and she cautioned me to never, ever, use them.

My clothes made me stand out even more. Since maman was a strict Catholic, she dressed us in classical, traditional clothes. Christel and I always wore braids and modest dresses.

I came to hate it. The other children pulled my braids.

#

During my first experience with school, I just wanted to be like the other children, to be accepted and not reminded that I was different. I wanted to forget about my past and start a new life in France, but I always felt that I was different from the other students, and being watched.

Even the way that you greeted people in France was at odds with what I was used to. Kissing as a greeting made me so uncomfortable, but my mother did it all the time. She held my head in her hands and gave me enthusiastic kisses on both cheeks, very loud and close to my ears. Her lips were like octopus suckers! Every time, I felt like the sound would break my eardrums.

Soon after I arrived, maman started to teach me good manners. Before every meal, I had to wash my hands and show them to her to prove that they were clean. I had a personalized napkin with a napkin ring to keep it between meals. If I wanted to push my food on the plate, I had to use a piece of bread, not my fingers, as was common in Cambodia. I had to keep my mouth closed when I chewed. I couldn't speak with my mouth full. I learned that it was impolite to cut others off when they spoke, and that I had to wait my turn. Rather than "I don't like this food," we were to say "I do not prefer this food." I must sit up straight at the table. I must not play with my food. I must wipe my mouth before drinking, to avoid leaving greasy marks on the edge of the glass. Even if I didn't like the food on my plate, I had to finish all of it. Often, I was the last to finish, because I didn't like the food, and I would just keep chewing the meat, unable to make myself swallow it. If we didn't want to finish something, maman would chide us for being impolite, and remind us that other people didn't have food to eat at all.

There were so many rules for me to learn, and it was so different from what I was used to.

On days off from school, maman taught catechism in our home to young children. Eric was in the group. I was not but I would discreetly listen to the lessons from my bedroom. Eric and I had not been baptized, so when the family went to church, he and I were not allowed to take communion. Instead we were assigned to collect the offering money in small baskets while other family members took communion. I often wondered about this and asked Christel how the communion wafer tasted. She would answer: "It has no taste. It's very dry and sticks to your tongue."

Finally, Eric went to be baptized. I asked maman to get baptized too. Maybe I just wanted to try the communion wafer and see how it tasted. But I was never actually baptized and never attended a catechism class.

I'm not sure why, but one thing that maman did not try to make me was a Christian. I never mentioned them to her, but I had brought with me some childish Cambodian spiritual beliefs, and in times of tension and sadness I fell back on them. I had conversations in my mind with spirits of my forebears—my natural father, for instance. I imagined that they were in the sky looking over me, protecting me, guiding me to make good decisions.

Another thing that divided me from French children was that I was shyer about my body. But in order to save water, I had to take baths with my sister Christel. It made me feel very uncomfortable. I didn't want to undress in front of anyone—in Cambodia you're always covered by a garment called a *sarong* or by a scarf called a *krama*. I remember trying to collect foam from the bath soap to hide my private parts, but after a while the bubbles would disappear and my naked body would be exposed.

For the first time in my life, I experienced cold weather. One day, maman told us to dress warmly and wear our woolen hats because it was going to snow. I got very worried. In the refugee camp at Song Be, I'd learned the French word for snow—*neige*—but because we didn't have an equivalent for it in Cambodian, it was translated as "ice" in that language. I didn't know that snow could be small and soft. I thought that ice cubes were going to fall on our heads!

I also began watching TV, and encountered more mystery. I'd seen a play or two on stage in Saigon, and in the refugee camp, some Charlie Chaplin silent films. The first thing I ever watched on French TV was a show about cowboys and indians where the main character was shot dead. I was so sad and scared! I began to cry because I thought he was dead for real. Days later, we watched another movie, about the life of Jesus Christ. I was astonished to find the same actor was playing one of the characters in the movie. I was confused and couldn't understand what had happened. Maman had to explain what an actor was, and that they didn't really kill people to make movies.

#

Though maman opposed any suggestion that I try to get in touch with my old family, she thought it would make me happy to have some reminders of Cambodia. She wanted to respect my culture and heritage.

Once, she had over to the house a Cambodian family who had lived in France for a very long time. Maman asked the mother to speak a bit of Cambodian with me. It was all very awkward.

But mostly, maman tried cooking sweet potatoes, rice and fish for the family, so I wouldn't miss Asian food. Though she meant well, I hated it. She overcooked the sweet potatoes, until the skin was falling apart. The rice was bad too. It was Uncle Ben's rice, American and pre-cooked, packaged in plastic bags that just had to be boiled. It was so bland. The rice I was used to in Cambodia was sticky and soft, and had a lovely fragrance. The fish we got from maman was always frozen white fish fillets, with a spongy texture, cooked with white cream. Cambodian fish was fresh and sweet, and smelled like spices and herbs.

But it was more than just the taste being wrong. The truth is, I didn't want to be reminded of Cambodia at all. I wanted to live in the present, and be like the other children. Every time she cooked Cambodian food, it only reminded me that I was different from everyone.

Yet though I wished to be French—and maybe even look European— it took me a long time to get used to French food. Especially the desserts. Cambodian cooking uses palm sugar, coconut milk and fruit, but it is often much less sweet than French desserts, especially the pastries. I was used to crisp, fresh flavors, not sugary sweets.

I sometimes got in trouble because of this. One day, my foster grandparents in Paris had us to their home for lunch. My grandfather had lovingly made a chocolate dessert for my family. It was far too sweet for me, but I had been taught it was rude not to eat all of it, so I tried my best. I ate tiny, tiny bites, and between I sipped water because otherwise I just couldn't swallow it. I was still going, forcing myself to eat tiny bite after tiny bite, long after the rest of the family had finished.

My grandfather asked me, "Do you like it?" To be polite, I responded, "Yes, Papy!"

He praised me for eating so delicately, and taking the time to fully appreciate the taste of the dessert. As a reward for the great compliment I had paid to his cooking, he gave me a second helping!

I was so embarrassed. I had no idea how I was going to finish it. My sister, who was sitting in front of me, discreetly glanced my way, trying not to burst out laughing. She knew what was really going on. I was saved when my grandparents went into the kitchen. Secretly, I gave the rest of my dessert to Christel.

In time, though, I did learn to like French cheese, especially the creamy, flowing kinds. Even the strong, smelly ones! In the morning, I particularly liked to melt Gruyère cheese into my hot tea, made from a Lipton tea bag. In Cambodia we use loose-leaf tea. Tea bags were an exotic concept to me; I continued to prefer the real flavor of a loose green tea.

#

In our household, we children could face punishment, though, unlike in Cambodia, it never involved physical blows. Punishment was often a strong reprimand followed by orders to go straight to our rooms. We might be forbidden to go out to play or see friends. There was an element of shame, of humiliation, because often maman would announce to our father, or grandparents, or even to her friends what we had done and how we were being punished. Sometimes I wondered if it was worse than receiving a whip.

The things that brought on punishment from my Catholic foster mother were very different from those that did from my Cambodian mother.

Rudeness was forbidden, and we were punished if we were caught using curse words. We were punished if we told lies, fought with each other, or stole from each other. Politeness and respect were very important to maman. We had to give her a good morning kiss when we woke up every day, and a goodnight kiss before we went to bed. We had to kiss her hello and goodbye when we went to school or returned home, and there was trouble if we didn't. Sometimes the offense could be as simple as giggling at the wrong time. Once Christel and I were banished to our rooms for doing that. Apparently we had made papa feel we were defying his authority.

Other strict rules applied to our behavior outside the house. There was no freedom to run around the neighborhood and play with the other children. Maman tracked our school schedules. We could never be late for school, and we had to come home straight afterwards.

My early childhood in Cambodia had entailed great freedom to come and go. Even in the Khmer Rouge years, I often went out on my own, or just with other children. We learned better and faster by experimenting ourselves, rather than obeying adults' words. Now I found maman's authority and rules severe. I began to resist and challenge her. I have always liked to know the reasons behind rules and punishments. If I don't see a good reason, I get upset and find it hard to accept and forgive. This meant that the language barrier was especially frustrating for me, because when things got tense, I sometimes found I didn't know French well enough to grasp my mother's explanation for why I was being punished, or the reason behind a rule.

It also hurt me that many of her rules did not apply to my classmates. For example, I wasn't allowed to ride a bike, though my classmates were. She told me many times that it was too dangerous, but many other students were riding bikes to school, and it never seemed dangerous to me.

-5-
Headstrong: Taking Control of My Life

In 1986, five years into my stay with my foster family, we moved to a new, bigger house. It was still in Roissy en Brie, but we children had to change schools. I stopped sharing a room with Christel, and got my own for the first time. In fact, we all got our own rooms, and we were allowed to choose the wallpaper and carpet color we wanted. Located above the garage, my bedroom was brightened nicely by a skylight.

We had a fireplace to warm up the main house and a small electric heater in each room. I always felt the cold more than the rest of my family, and sometimes after sitting still for hours studying, my feet and hands felt frozen stiff. We had a strict limit on the highest temperature we were allowed to keep our rooms. My mother enforced it, partially because she was often too warm, but also because electricity cost money. I was scared to set the heater at a comfortable temperature, in case she would burst in and scold me. Because of the cold, my skin was often dry. My lips, too, got dry and chapped easily, and sometimes cracked and bled. I never enjoyed winter, with its short, grey and depressing days.

But I never really compared the weather to Cambodia, or wished I was back in Cambodia because it was warmer. I think, as a defense mechanism, I tried to think of Cambodia as little as possible.

While I was in *lycée* (high school), doing my last three years of secondary education, the suburb we lived in started to take on an atmosphere of racism. It penetrated right into our own home, in fact. My older siblings Jean-François and Christel had by now gone to Paris to technical schools, and would return home for the weekends. Jean-François had begun to adopt a "skinhead" mentality and look. My brother, Ludovic, who still lived with us, started to follow his brother's lead. He dressed all in black, and wore heavy military-style boots called

"Doc Martens." He shaved his head and listened to weird, violent music. He started to get mean.

At first it was just words. If we happened to cross paths somewhere alone in the house, he would insult me. If I left the dinner table to get something from the kitchen, he would make some excuse to leave the table too and follow me, just to say hurtful things to me.

"You're like bad weeds! Pull them out and they just keep growing!" That line, the first time he said it, was so surprising. It cut me deeply and reminded me the Khmer Rouge period. His words have stuck with me ever since then.

"We fostered you," he would say, "and you haven't even brought us money for it!"

It was humiliating. I felt diminished every time he talked to me. I started to be afraid of him. Whenever I thought I might be alone with him, I got anxious. It was like torture. All I could do was to try and avoid him. I kept his treatment to myself, thinking that if I showed fear or cried, or told someone, he would take it as a victory, and push even harder. But as he tried and tried and got no response, his insults and threats became more intimidating. Still, I restrained myself and never replied, pretending to be calm and detached. I recalled the parting advice from Ma, my Cambodian mother, who had told me to make no trouble and put no burden on the people who would be looking after me, so I never told maman what was happening. I tried to find a positive space inside me instead, to pretend his words wouldn't hurt me. I'd often stay in my bedroom upstairs, and even though maman forbade us to lock our doors and sometime I would discreetly lock mine.

When we were in middle school, Ludovic was part of an exchange program by which students learned a foreign language. I studied English, but Ludovic studied German. One day, while he was at the bus stop, waiting for his German exchange students, he got into a fight with a young Asian man. I don't know what started it, but it ended with the Asian guy punching my foster brother hard in the stomach. Ludovic had to be sent to a hospital, and my parents filed a complaint with the local police.

After that, he treated me even more harshly. I wonder if he might have been trying to take revenge on me for that fight, substituting me for that other person since we were both Asian.

I also wondered how much of his reason was not because I was Asian, but because I got better grades than he did. Maman's parents were always telling us how important it was to study hard and get good grades, and they often praised me for my hard work at school. Ludovic might have resented that.

My relations with my brother Eric were also troubled.

Because I spoke no French when I arrived and had been kept back a grade, I was a whole grade below him, despite being only three months younger. Eric didn't study well. He often didn't take notes for homework, and forgot to study for exams or to turn in his projects. He was eventually made to repeat 8th grade (4ème in France). At that point, maman arranged for the two of us to be put in the same class so she could use me to better control his studies, for instance, consulting my study timetable when he refused to let her see his.

She set up a system of prizes that year, to reward good scores at school. If we got higher than 15 out of 20 on a project or test, we would get 5 francs (7 francs was the equivalent of one US dollar at the time). If we got 20 out of 20, we got 10 francs. She kept a notebook, and after she had verified our exam scores, she marked them down in the notebook. At the end of the month, we got our money. I made quite good money from this system, but it didn't work so well for Eric. The prize system didn't last long.

Eric had physically matured a lot by now. He had grown very tall, his voice had deepened, and he became quite handsome. He was very popular with the girls. He wasn't insolent, or a bad person, but he was very proud, and he paid more attention to his relationships than to his studies.

I sometimes wished that he would ask me for help more often. I wished too that I could be friends with him. But he never came to me for help. Maybe he believed I would report everything to maman. In the end, putting us in the same class didn't help him at all. It only made our relationship more awkward. I went on to higher education, and he started vocational training, like our other siblings.

Ludovic, meanwhile, continued his hostility. To cope, I returned to an old habit, which I had used as a child in Khmer Rouge Cambodia. When things get rough, I talk to myself. Nowadays, it's positive talk, that everything will be okay, or that I just need to be confident. But with Ludovic, it was about all the ways I could get revenge on him and make him respect me. I told myself over and over that he was going to be miserable, and I thought about all the ways I could make it happen.

But often I wondered if in fact I was the problem, or if there was something wrong with me. I never wanted to be a burden or a bother to them, but now my feelings were becoming very mixed about living in that family. I was grateful to them for fostering me, but I also wished I had been born in different conditions, where I didn't need to be adopted at all. On the worst days, I wished that I hadn't been born at all.

Looking back, I think I might have felt some survivor's guilt too, because I was fortunate enough to live in France with a foster family, while my biological family in Cambodia lived out of sight in poverty. So I restrained myself from complaining. But I had nobody to talk to about these things. My emotions just ended up troubling me and making me feel confused and alone.

As bad as things were with Ludovic, my biggest problems at home were disagreements with maman.

I had made a friend named Axelle. We had been classmates since grades 3 and 4 then she moved and now we were again at the same high school class and became neighbors. She was the second-oldest of five daughters, a very shy and gentle person, who helped her parents take care of her youngest sisters. She was also brilliant. She played the flute and clarinet. She always had the second or third highest marks in the class. I was doing well in science and math classes—a pattern that would hold throughout my education—but I never did as well in French and grammar as she, and so she helped me out.

She also had a bike, and she rode it freely. Sometime she would impress me by riding it "no-hands."

One time, Axelle and I were going off to another neighborhood to buy some ingredients for Asian food. It was a long trip, and so she brought her bike with her. When we were past the bushes behind my house, we thought we were far enough away that maman wouldn't see us. Then Axelle tried to teach me to ride. She sat on the back of the seat and balanced it for me while I pedaled in zig-zags down the cycling path. It was a bit scary but we had a lot of fun.

When we got home, maman asked if I had ridden the bike. I said no, because I thought she hadn't seen me. She got really angry and called me a liar. We hadn't been far enough away, and she had seen me. I felt so bad. I was ashamed that I had lied to her, but also upset that she had found me out. I felt like she might never trust me again.

Not only couldn't I ride a bike, I wasn't allowed to have friends come to the house. One time, when Axelle came anyway, my mother said, "My house is not a mall." Much later, when I was an adult, maman said she hadn't liked Axelle because she thought that she was a bad influence, turning me against her and making me rebellious.

Maman still didn't realize how embarrassing it was for me to go to school in dowdy, traditional clothes, with plastic decorations on my hair ties. Other students were wearing jeans and makeup and listening to pop music like Madonna and George Michael. They had started to flirt and go to parties (called *"une Boom"*) and kiss their boyfriends and girlfriends.

Despite all these controls, I managed to have a boyfriend, a fellow student at my high school. During the long summer vacation, he was away but had been writing to me, and sometimes telephoning the landline at my house to talk to me. Then, he suddenly stopped. I didn't know why. I thought he wanted to end our relationship, but didn't have the courage to tell me.

But when the next school year resumed, he told me that my mother had warned him not to contact me anymore and hung up on him. She had told him I had to focus on my studies.

Friends invited me to parties sometimes, and maman reluctantly let me go, but there were strict rules for that as well. I had to be home by 7 pm. The problem was that, for older teenagers, the party is only just starting at 7. Once, when I was 16 or 17, I was invited to a party at a friend's house. It was supposed to start at 5, but by 7 we were still waiting for all the guests to arrive. The doorbell rang. The host got up to open the door, thinking it was another guest.

It wasn't. My friend came back into the living room and announced to everyone that my mother was here to get me! One of my friends said, "Oh my god! It's only 7:15 and your mother is already here to pick you up?"

I was mortified. Most of my friends thought nothing of coming home from parties at midnight, or even one in the morning. My social life was ruined. What kind of boy would flirt with a girl whose mother had walked almost a kilometer (she didn't know how to drive) to get her from a party at 7:15 and with such a dark expression on her face?

Now that I look back on it, the whole incident is little bit funny. But at the time, of course, it was horrible. I was nearly finished high school, and the rules were the same as when I was in primary school.

I had another boyfriend. When I was 17, I began dating Laurent, a young, blond Polish-origin boy with dark green eyes. I knew he smoked weed, and I told him that it bothered me. He promised to stop if we were together.

The following summer, he convinced his parents to contact my mother, to invite me to their home for the summer vacation. Laurent had dropped out of school and still lived at his parents' house. To my great surprise, maman allowed me to go. The first evening I was there, his mother called him downstairs for a private discussion. Later, he told me that my mother, without my knowing, had sent a letter warning his parents of their responsibilities if something should happen, like if I became pregnant. His parents seemed worried and embarrassed, and so was I. Why couldn't she have talked to me instead of sending that letter? But of course, sex was a taboo subject in our family.

In French, an overprotective mother is called *"une mère poule,"* or a mother hen: someone who is overly worried that something might happen to her children. This was my mother. She needed to be in control of everything--where I went, who I went with, and what my relationships were like. I found it difficult to explain my feelings to her, or justify my actions. Her needing to know everything made me try to hide things from her. I was growing further and further away from her.

#

I still didn't talk about my life in Cambodia. Sometimes, when I felt lonely or sad, I replayed happy childhood memories in my mind. But I didn't think about actually going back. Despite my problems here in France, I felt I had left Cambodia for a brighter future.

Then, one day early in April 1990, that was all turned upside down: my oldest brother, Nguon, showed up unannounced at the gate of our house, with a few of our relatives. He had been stuck in a refugee camp for 11 years, but now had finally made it to France.

I was stunned to see him standing right in front of me. But I managed to stay calm. Despite all my efforts to suppress my past, it had finally caught up with me.

I felt like I should have been overjoyed to see my brother and relatives again after so long, but the truth is, I wasn't. I had been so young when I left that I hadn't really missed them. Now I got a full load of family news. Ma, Nguon told me, had been worried sick for years, because she had heard no news from me since I had gone to France. As soon as his documents had been approved, he'd come to France and started looking for me.

Nguon asked my foster parents if I could visit him in Paris suburbs where he was now living with Pou family members who'd been in the Song Be refugee camp.

I went. I met the relatives, and it was an odd and very complicated experience. Our interactions felt contrived, artificial. I didn't talk very much. These were family, this was my brother, but I hardly knew them, and I couldn't really think of them as family. The Pou's hadn't learned much French since arriving (they were too busy working). Nguon didn't speak much French either, so one of our other relatives had to translate.

Nguon didn't give up, though. That same year, in 1990, he took me to the pagoda at the Park de Vincennes in Paris. This was the place where the Cambodian community in France gathered at Khmer New Year. I had never been to the celebration since I moved to France. Usually, the Khmer New Year falls in mid-April (it moves around according to phases of the moon), and on that day back in 1990, spring had truly begun. It was a brilliant sunny day. The trees had begun to bud, and the flowers brightened the different corners of the park, while people took advantage of the first rays of sun to tan. Our family walked for a bit in the park. Nguon was surprised to see couples half-naked or in bikinis, exposing their bodies to the sun. In Cambodia, people cover their flesh to protect it from the sun. Being tanned is associated with doing agricultural work in the fields. Perhaps it reminded Nguon of the Khmer Rouge time. To remain white was preferable! Not only that, some couples were kissing languorously and lovingly. It was some real culture shock for Nguon—this was the first time he'd seen people kissing in public. He was so surprised that he took photos of them. Embarrassed, I asked him to stop. I told him that it was just how things were in France.

Traditional Cambodian music was playing through loudspeakers. All my relatives were so excited and joyful to be meeting again. We sat together on a giant mat on the grass and shared Cambodian dishes and desserts. Most people there didn't speak Cambodian as I'd expected, but a dialect of Chinese. The festival was full of all kinds of people—not just Cambodian, but Chinese, and some non-Asian people as well.

My brother tried to take the place of Ma, our mother. He wanted me to sit with my legs folded like Cambodian women would traditionally do, to peel fruit for others, serve them with both hands, and behave in all the ways he considered correct and traditional for a proper Cambodian lady. Nguon insisted that I learn to address all my many relatives in the traditional Khmer and Chinese way: depending on how they were related to me, and whether they were on my mother's or father's side. He corrected my manners in front of them, which I found embarrassing. He was treating me like a child, like I hadn't grown up since the Song Be refugee camp. Besides, I did not feel I was a Cambodian. As far as I was concerned, I had become a French girl! I didn't see my relatives often, so how could I remember all the terms that Nguon wanted me to learn? I just called my relatives by their first names. To my brother, I was extremely disrespectful. He also faulted me for not keeping up with Cambodian language.

#

Back at home, I was pressing on with education. I had completed grade 11 and sat for the French language component of the *"Bac."* I was accepted for grade 12—my last year of high school—with only few points "short" to make up in the Bac. There was an impressive difference between my marks in the two parts of the test. In my French oral test, I got 17/20, but in my written test only 5/20.

At the oral, I had to explain a passage from the book "An Iceland Fisherman" by Pierre Loti, which we had studied during the year in class. I remember feeling very inspired by the book and its strong emotions, like the love of the fishermen for the sea, and at the same time for their wives, and the unequal struggle between those loves. The passage I had to explain was about being torn between sea and land, which included the women waiting patiently with their eyes constantly turned towards the blue waters. At the end, the sea was victorious, as a vicious tempest took away the fisherman from their cherished families. I could see and feel so clearly all the emotional themes through the images and metaphors Loti used. I think that the examiner was impressed by my explanations. Perhaps my inner sensibility, my buried emotions and my separation from my natural family had developed into a skill for perceiving feelings, a sort of emotional intelligence.

#

At home, things were getting worse. Once during one of our arguments, maman told me "Until the day you turn 18, you live under my roof, and under my rules!" After that, I could take my "click and clack," which meant my belongings, and leave home! It was at first surprised by this statement, which felt like an ultimatum. But after turning it over in my mind, I chose to see it as light at the end of the tunnel. This was how frustrated I had become with life in this house. I would reach 18, and then I would leave.

And I had learned of serious problems my foster father was having. I overheard papa and maman arguing in the garage, where they went thinking the children wouldn't hear. But now I learned that papa had started to drink. Later, Christel told me details: he was hiding liquor in the garage and empty beer bottles under the car seat. I began noticing that papa would always have some wine with dinner, and some with lunch when he was home on weekends. Maman had started to water down his wine. If she couldn't persuade him to stop drinking, she could at least try to reduce the amount of alcohol he was taking in. But he was angry at her for it.

Of course I didn't say anything. I knew maman would get angry if I brought it up. She always liked to keep up appearances.

It all reached its climax in my penultimate year of high school. I didn't like arguments, but one day maman and I blew up at each other. I can't remember exactly what it was about, but I was upstairs and she was downstairs, and we were shouting back and forth. "I'm fed up with this family!" I screamed. She got very angry and ran upstairs to catch me. She dragged me into the bathroom, ran cold water in the sink, and—I was flabbergasted at this—forced my head under the tap. She felt it would calm me down.

She was a large woman, much bigger than me, and I couldn't get free! I struggled hard against her strong grip. I just wanted to get my head out of the sink. Then she let me go. Terrified, I turned around to look at her. Her face was violent purple, and she was gasping for breath.

We both realized that things had gone totally out of control. She went back downstairs, got her breath back, and soon I was hovering over her, asking her if she was all right, if she was badly hurt, and trying to make her more comfortable.

Years later she told me that she realized that day that I didn't really dislike her, and I wasn't a bad person. Rather, I was frustrated and upset. The fight was a turning point for her understanding of me.

But she nonetheless concluded that it would be best for both of us if I lived somewhere else. If I stayed, we would only argue more, and make each other more unhappy.

So I had reached the light at the end of the tunnel. I accepted her decision. I did not want to remain in this house long-term. But I couldn't help feeling that staying would have been better for my goals of education. Switching schools between 11th and 12th grade was not a good idea.

#

Maman, in her organized way, started exploring how I could move to somewhere else in the foster system.

But before I left, she set up psychological counseling for me. Back then, in France, seeing a psychologist had a very negative connotation. I was very worried. Did she think I was mentally ill? Was I mentally ill? I asked all my close friends. Did they think I was weird, or even a little crazy?

I went to the psychologist. We talked about the troubles I had with maman and my guilt as a foster child about bringing more trouble to the family. He told me that if my foster parents had difficulties, it was not my fault. If they had brought me into their home, it was for their happiness as well as mine. I shouldn't feel responsible for decisions they made. This was the first time someone had told me this. It felt re-assured. Up until then, I had been feeling guilty about everything. Still, I didn't mention Ludovic's bullying, because I worried it might bring my parents trouble. I had always taken to heart my biological mother's advice to not add a burden on people. I had worried my foster parents might regret hosting me, but the psychologist made it much easier for me. I felt a lot more gracious toward my French family after that. That guilt lifted a bit.

#

Since arriving in France, I had suffered from a skin rash. Doctors had been unable to find a physical explanation, so psychological ones were offered. Perhaps it was from stress, either from the Khmer Rouge era or from my time in the refugee camps. But certainly my first years in France could have contributed too.

As an adolescent and young adult, I felt a need for more affection and nurturing than I was getting. I wanted hugs and close relationships. I was more sensitive and, I think, compassionate than most of the children and adults around me, too, and yet at times I struggled with uncontrolled sorrow and anger. I cried when I was alone. I had a desire to escape from the complications of life. It was always worse when something happened at home to make me feel suffocated. I questioned the meaning of it all. Where was my life heading?

Looking back now with more experience and understanding, I know that maman did not have any bad intent. Like any mother (and like Ma in the old days) she was trying with limited resources to raise me to succeed, to give me the best chances in life. From her military father, she had inherited very strict rules by which children must obey parents and not question their authority. That was the only way she knew. Unfortunately, it meant I and my siblings never had a chance to make her understand that her methods could have the opposite effect on us. It didn't help us grow and deal with our emotions in a healthy way, or approach the real, harsh world in the best prepared manner.

But I will say that the strict education and household rules of those years with the foster family contributed to who I am today, in a good way. I don't think it works for everyone: my foster siblings were raised in the same way, and they didn't end up with the same drive and motivation that I had. By the time I parted ways with my foster family, I feel I had become a resilient young woman, with a healthy lifestyle. I never was attracted to drugs, cigarettes or alcohol. Despite our fights, I had made maman proud.

For my development in this period I must give credit too to my brother Nguon and his sometimes hectoring style. Thanks to him, I began to slowly reconnect with my origins, even if I didn't want to. At the time, I felt that what he was trying to teach me wasn't relevant—I preferred to be a French girl. But he started me on the path that eventually led to me being proud to be Cambodian.

I had two or three sessions in total with the psychologist. Then it came time to leave my foster family.

-6-
Keeping on Track in a Tough Foster Hostel

Shortly after my last day of Grade 11, a small white pick-up truck arrived at the family house. At the wheel was Philippe, education manager at La Haute Bercelle hostel, run by the French foster system. It was located in Fontainebleau, about 50 kilometers away. I was waiting, wearing a classic, fuchsia skirt and a white lace blouse. My belongings and a guinea pig that I had rescued from the school laboratory were loaded aboard. Only maman was there to see me off. I avoided her eyes. By now I just wanted to get moving.

I felt shy and uncomfortable as I stepped through the hostel's door for the first time. As Philippe introduced me to the hostel's cook and some of the other people who worked there, a girl named Sophie came down to meet me. She was a tall black girl, with a boyish style.

Once I had been introduced, Sophie stood above me on the staircase and asked me what grade I was in.

"1st S," I told her – "S" stood for "Sciences."

"Being around people like you gives me hives," she replied.

I was beginning to understand. This was a place for young women who were attending school but had serious emotional problems with family, studies, and people in general. My foster parents had chosen it without consulting me.

I would soon understand too that Sophie was the unofficial leader of the hostel's band of girls. Smart and respected, she had lived there the longest. It was hardly a friendly welcome that she gave me that first day, yet she and the others did try to bring me into their group. On an evening soon after my arrival, I was asked to join them in Sophie's bedroom, where they were listening to Bob Marley and preparing marijuana joints. Smoking and drinking were of course not allowed in the hostel.

And of course it happened anyway. Our supervisors knew, but they could never catch the girls in the act—they only found the empty bottles or the lingering smell of weed. Sophie, the most daring and intimidating girl in the place, was often the one who brought in the marijuana, which she bought from her boyfriend and other contacts. She knew all the staff there and usually smoked when there was a lax one on duty.

In her room, I sat in a circle with them. Sophie was the chief—she took the first puff from the joint and passed it to the next girl. This spooked me, but I was not going to go along with their nonsense to please them. When it was my turn, I told them honestly that I didn't even know how to smoke a regular cigarette, so I was certainly not going to smoke marijuana. That was the end of me as a member of their group.

I knew marijuana was a drug, bad for your health, as well as illegal. But I didn't want to be a bad roommate or create problems by getting the others into trouble, either. So I didn't report them, though I would have said what I knew if asked. I just wanted to focus on my own goals of finishing high school and moving on to higher education.

I shared a bedroom with another girl named Tina, who was half Portuguese. She was quite beautiful. She dyed her hair blonde, and was attending a hairdressing school. However, she was sometimes frustrating to live with. Everything had to be dusted meticulously. Even if we were in bed, about to go to sleep, if she saw a fleck of dust under the furniture, she would have to get up and clean it. She cried often and sometime I could hear her sobbing at night. Her family life had been quite bad. She was beaten by one of her parents, who was an alcoholic, and then later was beaten by her boyfriend. Despite all this, she was the gentlest girl of the group.

We were all required to dine together according to the hostel's fixed schedule. We all had tasks to do. We took turns setting the table for dinner, washing the dishes, taking out the garbage, going shopping with the cook, sweeping the floor. Every two weeks we received a small stipend.

If we did well in our studies, budgeted wisely, followed the rules and showed general responsibility and maturity, we could move to the next level of independence, life in an apartment shared with another girl.

Sadly the typical girl at the hostel had many detours before she reached that destination, assuming she got there at all. The reasons why were on display at dinner, which we took with whichever educator was on duty.

Sophie sat at the head of the long dinner table. At her side was her friend and acolyte, a short but imposing Algerian girl. Sophie usually had first choice of the best piece of meat (her acolyte even saved it for her if she was late). After that, it was every girl for herself. People pushed to grab the best remaining pieces and French fries. They filled only their own plates, paying no attention to others. Respect and good manners were almost nonexistent. They talked to each other rudely. There was no "please" or "thank you."

Arguments broke out at a moment's notice; sometimes I feared for my physical safety. One girl might accuse another of losing her make-up or taking her latest fashionable clothes. Shouting erupted, insults flew. Any educator who tried to intervene would get cursed. Threats of punishment would often only escalate the conflict. Usually it ended that the girl announcing she wouldn't listen to the educator preach at her anyway. She would walk out, slamming the door. This took a toll on the staff too. Sometimes they retreated to their own rooms to calm down.

At times like this, I wondered how maman could have sent me to a place like this. Did she really know what it was? Was this some kind of psychological stratagem to demonstrate how great her home was and get me to telephone and beg to be taken back?

But I don't mean to suggest that life at the hostel was all trouble. The staff educators were kind, communicative, and attentive, with psychological training to listen to us. We were all assigned one with whom we could discuss our problems and concerns. Mine was a woman named Dominique, and I came to be quite close to her. She and her new partner were passionate about flea markets, and sometimes during her days off, she would take me out for a weekend going through flea markets with them. She cared for me like a mother and a best friend.

And on the weekends, the educator manager, Phillipe, often organized outings. Once, we went riding mountain bikes in hilly paths of the Fontainebleau forest. I told him honestly that I barely knew how to ride a bicycle, so I'd have to pass up this activity. He insisted, and the other girls looked at me weirdly, surprised, I think, that someone of my age couldn't ride a bike. I didn't want to look prissy and straight-laced, so I gave in. As we rode off, I was silently blaming maman for keeping me away from bikes.

Soon we were going up and down rough, hilly paths between big trees. I became nervous, and scared. I couldn't keep the bike stable. I was going downhill too fast, with jerky movements. Suddenly we came across a big, tall rock in the middle of the path. The others went around it, but I, panicking, braked abruptly and was thrown off the bike, clean over the rock. I landed three or four meters away on the dirt and leaves! Luckily, I was only bruised, with some rips in my trousers. As I recovered from the shock, I had more thoughts about maman, recalling her warnings about biking being dangerous.

I could also escape on weekends to Nguon's apartment in Paris. But that often meant a different kind of tension. We had very different views on what I should do with my life. I was still dating Laurent, the Polish boy, and once Nguon found contraceptive pills in my belongings. He quizzed me about them. He told me that I shouldn't have a French boyfriend. French men, he said, didn't make good husbands, because they were often alcoholics and smokers. I was upset that he could believe such a stereotype.

Once he even told me that from back in Cambodia Ma had arranged for me to marry her best friend's son, who had emigrated to Australia after the Khmer Rouge regime. My brother showed me a recent photograph of him. It was a very weird feeling for me. Did Nguon really expect me to show interest just from this one photograph? Would he expect me to move to Australia, just to marry a stranger? I was quick to tell him that I was extremely sure I didn't want to have a relationship, or any contact at all, with this boy.

#

Through all of this, I managed to remain a diligent and responsible girl. I earned the trust of the hostel's director quickly. After about a year at the hostel, when I was in Grade 12 (terminale D in France) at the Francois 1er high school in Fontainebleau, I was allowed to move to an apartment in the neighboring town of Avon. There I would live with a girl named Brigitte. There was no guinea pig in the transfer this time; it had expired at the hostel.

I didn't hear about it at the time, but recently maman told me that during my time at the hostel she confidentially contacted the director to ask how I was doing. He told her that he wished every girl could be like me. I was "a perfect example," he said.

My foster grandmother told me later I'd made a good choice leaving home (to the other family members, maman depicted my departure as my idea). She had been worried, because my brother Eric had turned to drugs. Poor Grandma! She did not know what kind of kids I was close to at La Haute Bercelle. I was offered free cannabis!

Fontainebleau was a better-off town, a "bourgeois city." It hosted a large military base. The high school was "Lycée François 1er," considered to be one of the best in the country, and it was mostly for rich children. I was the only non-white student in my class. (My fellow hostel girls attended other schools, mostly vocational ones). The place where I was now living, Avon, was a less fancy area, and further away from the high school. I had to change buses to get there. Now that I lived in an apartment, I had to do my own shopping, cooking and laundry, as well as my studies. There wasn't much time for anything else.

But during my school breaks, I did find time to work at a holiday center for children in the suburb of Villejuif, south of Paris. My foster cousin was the director there, and had helped me get the job. I saved my pay toward getting my driver's license. I passed a test to be a certified leader of a youth holiday camp. It would make me a more attractive candidate for future camp jobs.

In Grade 12, I got a taste of the affluent life. I became friendly with a classmate named Alexandra, and she invited me to her family's large house with a barn in Fontainebleau, or to their country house in Picardy in the north of France. She was the third oldest in a family of five children, and her family was quite wealthy. Her two brothers were at an elite military high school, and her younger sister was at a private school reserved for children of members of the Legion of Honor. Like in maman's family, both of her parents had military backgrounds, but the family resemblance ended there.

Alexandra had several horses and took care of them with the help of her mother. She was an avid rider, and sometimes competed in races.

I rode a horse for the first time with her. I did not enjoy the experience.

This is how it happened. One school holiday, I was with the family at their house in Picardy. They had brought along a retired mare from the French cavalry that her parents had just bought for her. Alexandra was teaching her younger sister and some other children how to ride horses in a field near the house. One by one, they took turns on the mare. Alexandra told me to give it a try. I said yes.

At first, she held the mare's reins and everything was fantastic.

"See how easy it is?" she asked.

Then, she let go of the reins and told me I could manage on my own.

The mare began to accelerate until finally she was galloping! She ran like a fury back towards the house. By now I was lying forward on her back, clutching her mane because I had lost hold of the reins and couldn't control her. I saw the road ahead and knew I couldn't stop her. I was sure that a car would hit us! In a panic, I jumped off her back.

That's where Alexandra found me, and helped me back to the house.

The mare had stopped when she reached the house. Alexandra's mother saw the horse without a rider and immediately realized that something was wrong. We arrived home, despite my limping and having several bruises, including one from the mare's hoof, and a big hole in my pants from the fall. I said it was nothing, that I was fine. Still, Alexandra's mother blamed her for the incident, and scolded her harshly in front of us. I felt sorry for Alexandra.

That evening during the dinner with the rest of the family, Alexandra's father asked me a lot of questions about my background and my family. There returned that old feeling of being scrutinized, of being an outsider. I didn't feel comfortable talking about my past to people I had only just met. I answered his questions to be polite. Jokingly, I asked him if he was working for the police.

I hadn't meant to be insulting, but it was immediately clear that he wasn't happy with me. There was a cold and quiet moment, then Alexandra's mother changed the subject. I thought the other children were surprised—perhaps none of them were used to talking to their father that way. Alexandra's father, after all, had a high rank in the military, and led a troop in Fontainebleau. Afterwards, I realized that maybe I had been rude, or too bold.

The next day Alexandra initiated me into windsurfing in a lake. She made sketches in a notebook to help me understand how to recognize the direction of the wind and harness its force to move forward, at the same time using our legs, our bodies, and hands to keep the board on course. Once we arrived at the end of the lake, she said, we would come back up against the wind by doing zigzags. One of her brothers was buzzing around in a small motorboat on the lake and, if we had any problem, he would tow us.

Then came the practice. I struggled hard to stay balanced on my board but several times ended up diving into the lake. I'd climb back again on my board, with the sail covered with water and my arms not strong enough to lift it up. Again, splash! Alexandra made it look so easy and fun. I wanted to please her. At last, miraculously, I brought everything together and the wind blew me to the other end of the lake! Her brother came to the rescue and towed me back.

Another day, on a big deserted beach, I watched her brother taming the wind force and gravity with a sand yacht. He was moving really fast along the shore, making the seagulls flee with fear, when he suddenly turned around on two wheels like a stuntman. Stopping at our side, he kindly asked if I wanted to give it a try.

"No thanks!" I had had enough of new sports.

Back at the house, I helped Alexandra's mother set the table for our breakfast, put lids away, and wash the dishes, even though they didn't ask me but that was a way to show gratitude for having me in vacation with them. Maman had taught me good manners. I was usually appreciated for my good manners and being a nice person!

#

That year on my final Bac exams I didn't succeed in getting an average total score of 10/20, the requirement for passing. I did well in sciences, but social sciences—literature, philosophy, history—continued to hold me back. I would have to repeat grade 12. This was an emotional body blow to me, but I managed to put it in perspective: I had had a tumultuous year, moving to the hostel, but now things were settling down and I would do better in my studies.

Alexandra went ahead, but there was only one other girl in my class who was repeating grade 12: Aurelie, who was a little tomboyish. She and I became very close. Her father was a ranking officer of the parachute division at Fontainebleau. Being an only child, she was quite spoiled. In her last year of high school, she got a BMW. Her father sometimes took her skydiving, where she got to flirt with the soldiers.

In the forest, she taught me how to drive her BMW. Once, I almost demolished it. I was driving, suddenly got scared, and in my panic pressed the brake and accelerator at the same time. The car was heading straight for a giant tree! Thankfully Aurelie pulled up the hand brake before we could crash. We sat there for a moment, pale and shocked, before we managed to drive home.

Later, in 1992, I passed my driving exam and got my license.

My other classmates were all of privileged backgrounds, with well-off, caring parents. Most seemed headed for success in life. If they were struggling with a subject, well, the parents hired a tutor.

I was friends with Alexandra and Aurelie, but for the most part I isolated myself at that school, finding excuses to reject invitations because I didn't have the money. I didn't want to be the one who always had to be helped. Still, I think most people at the school liked me. Sometimes I would briefly imagine I had a life like theirs, in a harmonious foster family with nurturing parents, where I could feel safe and free.

School pressure mounted. In the French system, you only get two chances to pass a grade. If I failed again, I'd have to drop out or move to another kind of school. I could not face that idea. I knew I had to study harder.

I had been talking to Nguon about my difficulties in school, telling him I was worried I wouldn't pass the final exams. He told me he could get me a job. At the time, he worked in a "Chinese" butcher shop in Paris. He had a few connections among the Chinese community in Paris (which in fact was a combination of people from China, Cambodia, Vietnam, Laos and Thailand). Most of the people who worked in Chinese stores were immigrants who got jobs immediately after arriving in France in order to survive.

If I took up Nguon's offer, I'd be working with people who didn't speak much French, which would be a problem, since I'd forgotten most of my Khmer and didn't speak their dialect of Chinese either. These were retail jobs, which wouldn't lead to a career I wanted. The wages were very low, so I couldn't have afforded to study while I worked. I knew too that it was common practice not to declare some workers to avoid paying taxes, and I was afraid that this would be found out and threaten my refugee status. So I told Nguon I'd had made up my mind—I would study harder than ever to get a good marks in the exams.

After a year and a half of separation from my foster family, I somewhat reluctantly decided to attend a family reunion, celebrating my maternal grandparents' fiftieth wedding anniversary. The celebration took place at the Voisin le Bretonneux castle, about 25 kilometers from Paris, which belonged to the Paris fire fighters and had been turned into a hotel and restaurant for members of that service.

In the garden at the party, I approached maman and papa to greet them. But the first thing maman did was ask, ironically: "So, you don't smoke or drink alcohol?" She assumed I had fallen under the influence of the other girls at the hostel. I was offended and disappointed. In my mind, she still didn't know me, and didn't appreciate that I was old enough to understand right from wrong and make healthy choices.

Her tone cut short my attempt to talk to her and reconnect. I walked away silently. The time to make peace had not yet arrived.

#

Again I took the Bac exam. The day the results were due out, Aurelie drove me to the university where they would be posted. When she saw her name in the list of successful candidates, she was ecstatic. This was her pass to go to university!

My name was not on the list. My final average score had been under 10 out of 20. I felt so stupid for doing so badly even after repeating my 12th grade! There was a saving grace, though: I hadn't completely failed. I would get one more chance to take the exams. I could select two subjects on which I thought I could improve from the previous exams, and make up the missing points. But I had lost my confidence. My inner voice was telling me that I would surely fail. It was a nightmare. I had never been so desperate in my life. What would I do with myself if I didn't get my Bac after that second round? My allowance from the French state agency for social affairs would be cut off, too, once I reached the age limit.

To add to my unhappiness, I was having trouble around this time with Laurent because of a long distance relationship. He was living in the east of France. I knew he had taken up cigarettes and weed again.

All of these things went through my mind when I saw my score. But Aurelie couldn't contain her excitement, and immediately phoned her father.

Suddenly, in the middle of an animated, joyful conversation with him, she handed the phone to me. I was surprised—I had barely met him, and couldn't remember ever having a conversation with him. But right there on the phone, he proceeded to give me a big speech, like the father or coach I had never had. He told me that I hadn't lost the battle—you've never lost until you've used up your last chance. As a high-ranking military officer, it seemed he really knew how to give a motivational speech. I felt so fortunate to have him there to give me that talk at just the right time, to know that someone I barely knew nevertheless cared about me enough to try to help me. He gave me hope and the courage to go back and keep trying, and trust in myself to the end.

I listened to him, and with tears in my eye promised him I would go back to my apartment and spend the few days remaining before the second round studying as hard as I could. I would do my absolute best.

So I studied morning to evening. I redid exams on which I hadn't done well. I stopped studying only long enough to eat. And I passed! To this day, I feel that the miracle of the pep talk from Aurelie's father is what got me through.

#

Aurelie went on to a traditional full course of study at the University of Paris. I couldn't do that, however. My marks in the Bac weren't good enough for a scholarship, and when my state stipend ran out, I'd have to find money somewhere. University in France was nearly free at the time, but textbooks were quite expensive—too expensive. So I chose a two-year course to become a laboratory technician. It was offered at the Medical Laboratory School, part of the educational institution south of Paris's 13th district known as ENCPB, les Gobelins. I was confident that with the degree in hand, I'd be able to find a medical lab job that was interesting, would keep challenging my intellect—and let me continue to study while I was working.

I moved to a university residence in Saint Denis, north of Paris. However, the ENCPB was in the south of Paris, so I spent a lot of time in trains and subways. It was a two-hour trip each way, but I couldn't live any closer—apartments near the university were far too expensive.

When it came time for my final exam, another crisis arose. I got anxious, nervous of failing, and so doubted my ability that I could not think fast and straight. I did not pass. And so again I repeated a year and this time I passed. I got the Brevet of Advanced Technician in 1995 and started working in the same year.

My first job in a medical lab was part-time at CMETE, a private medical laboratory specializing in tropical diseases. The lab was located in Paris's 1st District. The company had contracts with big drilling and petroleum companies. Before being sent abroad, employees of these companies had to go through a medical check-up at CMETE. Then they had follow-up inspections once or twice a year.

I was hired as a temporary substitute for regular employees who were on parental leave or taking summer vacations. I continued to study, so I'd have a better chance of getting future jobs in medical labs. The following year, I obtained a certificate for drawing blood samples.

Later on, the blood certificate and my driving license helped me get a permanent position at a private medical laboratory called Gendrault Mancy Tallobre. It was located in a wealthy part of Paris's 7th District, Rue du Bac. Compared to CMETE, this lab had quite a different atmosphere. It catered to music and TV celebrities and former big politicians, as well as a convent and a private plastic surgeon who had a practice on the Champs Élysées. Often clients would have us come to their homes to take blood samples—that's why having a driving license helped me get hired.

I had a good job now, but again I did not see my education as complete. I asked to work the early morning schedule so that I could attend a graduate class on cell biology and microbiology at the Conservatoire National des Arts et Métiers in Paris.

#

I was 24 years old when I had my first palm reading. It was 1995 and I was friends with a Thai student who was on a scholarship in Paris to study mechanical engineering. We lived on the same floor at the university residence. When we both had free time, we would spend it with each other. We'd often prepare food together, or I would show him Paris and where to find Asian food.

One day, I saw that he had a book with a diagram of a hand and palm on it, with many lines and annotations. I was surprised and curious. I asked what he was doing with such a book.

He said he was not an expert, but he could give me a palm reading.

So he studied the lines on my hand and announced that I would go back to Cambodia (which turned out to be true). He made a few other predictions, too. The one that resonated the most with me was that I would die young.

Even though I'd never believed in fortune-telling or palm readings, I was quite disturbed by this one. I couldn't believe that my friend would tell me such a horrible fate. That prediction did not come true, since I am 45 as I write this, but I nonetheless think the reading did me a lot of good. Perhaps thinking I might die young helped me be enthusiastic and energetic about life, and to achieve my goals quickly. If it was possible that I might die young, I wanted to make sure to live a life without regret!

—Part Three—

Back to my Roots

-7-
Reunion with My Lost Family

In 1995, I was still working at CMETE and taking evening classes in cellular biology. Cambodia seemed very far away, to the extent I thought about it at all. Then one day, my siblings there got in touch with Nguon. Ma had been diagnosed with diabetes. She might have been suffering from it already for years. The prognosis was not good. She did not have long to live.

Nguon, his family and I decided to take a month during summer vacation to go see them. To me the time seemed right for a reunion. I'd now been separated for 15 years from Ma and the other family members who had remained behind. Yet, recalling the difficulties of bonding again with Nguon, I got on the plane with some apprehension.

Nguon and I still held refugee status in France, and were not officially allowed to return to Cambodia using our travel documents. So we flew to Ho Chi Minh City, formerly Saigon, in Vietnam. There the reunion took place.

Ma's diabetes was at an advanced stage, and her vision was blurry, but she still recognized me as soon as she saw me. She called out my name and reached for my hands with tears of joy and nostalgia in her eyes. Soon, I was in tears as well. Everyone was.

I was surrounded by family members. It seemed they could not get enough of holding me, touching me, and looking at me! They wanted me to update them on everything that had happened in the fifteen years we'd been separated. They asked about even the smallest details about my life. I felt overwhelmed.

Eyes red, we spent those first hours exchanging news. It was a laborious process, because despite Nguon's urgings, I hadn't re-learned the Khmer language. Nguon and Chhay had to translate for me. Without them, I could only understand body language.

I was surrounded by old family members, and there were many new ones too! I had new little nieces and nephews to meet. Heang was now married and had three daughters (Maeve, Sokyou and Chou). My brother Chhay had one daughter (Seav Houng) and a son (Lucky).

Our meeting felt natural for my family, but I wasn't emotionally prepared for quick re-integration. I think that after the first moments, when we were all crying, I became a bit distant to them. I wasn't able to fully respond to their affection and constant hugs. I felt uncomfortable. I had spent the many years in France trying to become independent and contained. I had become very accustomed to holding in my feelings. To me, my Cambodian relatives were a "new" family, and I felt I needed to keep a little separation from them. Here I was with my own family, who wanted me to feel I was at home again and that I was always loved, though they were from a culture that I had left behind. There was an inner conflict between my rational mind and emotional self.

That night, we all slept on mats together. I found it awkward to sleep close to so many people.

Like Nguon, the rest of my family wanted me to be a traditional Cambodian woman. In Cambodian culture, it is disrespectful to point your feet towards someone as you sit. Instead, people bend their knees and tuck their feet underneath them, so that their feet are always pointing away from the group. My brothers kept correcting me about how I sat, but I just couldn't stay in that position very long. My muscles cramped up.

They also expected me to be docile and obliging, to serve food to the older members of the family, and to cut fruit for them. But I couldn't even peel fruit the way they wanted—I peeled them in the French way, upside down or towards my body, instead of away from my body like a Cambodian would.

My sister-in-law, Soar, was often held up as the perfect example that I should follow. I started to grow annoyed and tired with all the rules, morals and manners they expected me to adopt. They were treating me like a child again!

One of the few things in which I took real pleasure during this visit was the food. There was always something wonderful to eat. I rediscovered scents and flavors that took me back to childhood times in Cambodia after the Khmer Rouge. We slurped the traditional Cambodian soup samlor kako flavored with vegetables and fruit like green papaya, pea eggplant and bitter melon leaves. There was lots of fresh fish too—so much better than what I got in France. How I remember the coconut milk, the sweet aroma of lemongrass, the grilled rice.

The days crept by. I silently yearned to go out and explore this country Vietnam on my own. However, I did my best to pretend I was enjoying myself. Ma was so happy to be reunited with us. She had only a short time left to live, so I wanted her to have good memories of this trip.

The whole experience was culture shock all over again, just like when I'd first moved to France. I wished the time would go faster and I would fly home to France and normalcy as soon as possible.

#

There was one particular story that I heard on that visit that stuck with me. My brother Chhay told me that when he was young, he had wanted to study medicine and become a physician. He had found a company that said they would help him with the paperwork to go to Russia to study. But after he'd paid his fee, they made off with his money and never contacted him again.

The Khmer Rouge had been intensely anti-intellectual and had killed many Cambodian intellectuals—sometimes even killing people just because they wore glasses. This had crippled the Cambodian education system, especially the universities. Cambodia didn't have institutions to allow its people to realize their potential or dreams or vocation, such as studying medicine.

It made me realize how lucky I was to have gone to France, where I got a good education at almost no cost. And despite the cultural distance that I felt with my old country, Chhay's story got me thinking I should do something for people there, although I didn't yet know what.

To start, though I would need to overcome the language barrier with my natural family. So when I returned to France, I enrolled in a Mandarin class in Paris' Chinatown. I could have studied Khmer, but I thought Mandarin would be more helpful for getting a job, and my family would more or less understand me in that language.

When I arrived to enroll in the class, which was conducted in the church area of Chinatown, I met a man named Pierre. He was standing outside the school. Politely, he gestured for me to go in ahead of him.

We were placed in the same Mandarin class—the one for beginners. Soon I noticed that this white guy was talented. It seemed like he understood every lesson almost instantly. He sat in the back of the class, and I sat in the front, so we didn't talk much at first, but I was very impressed whenever he answered questions. After a while, he befriended one of the other students, who was a classmate friend of mine, and through him, we started talking.

Later, he told me that he had seen me that first day, noticed my elegance and my "beautiful smile," and had deliberately signed up for the class I was in, rather than the higher level class that he should have been in, in the hopes of getting to know me.

At the time, Pierre was doing French military service as a document translator for the fire fighters. But he had lived for a long time outside France, in Thailand and Canada, and travelled in other countries of Southeast Asia. He had a girlfriend, from Hong Kong, who had recently moved to Canada. But still Pierre and I became friends.

#

At around this time, Laurent and I finally broke up. We were just very different people. He was attending vocational education, doing an

82

apprenticeship as a pastry chef, while I was pursuing higher education. He failed frequently in school and at his work, but instead of getting upset or working harder, he would just shrug and continue as before. His siblings often called him a loser, and he took out his anger and frustration in violence and vices. He smoked marijuana and drank hard liquor. I strongly disapproved, and I told him so. Some of our conversations got very tense.

I might have come to an understanding with him if he had just told me what he was doing, but he would smoke and then lie to me about it, even though I could smell it on him. For me, the dishonesty was worse than the actual vice.

That Christmas and New Year were lonely for me. Dealing with a breakup at that time of year is worse than at any other time, I think. All the other families are celebrating. You constantly see happy couples in the streets, and the decorations remind you that you should be close to your loved ones.

Pierre knew that I was having a tough time with the breakup, and he did what he could to help. As well as being a translator, he also volunteered on weekends as a fire guard at a theatre, so he could get free entry to the shows. He offered to take me to see a play, and I accepted.

Pierre's father had died a few weeks after we met. We helped each other, and he touched my soul by telling me that he had written about me in letters to his father, which had been a great help to him.

Pierre was much more like me than Laurent was. He already knew a lot about Asia, from travelling and living there. Education was important to both of us, and he supported my study efforts. We wanted very similar things: to work in a job that improved the lives of others, to try and make a better world, and to travel. He was also from a similar background to mine—at least on the French side of things. His parents were Catholic. His mother considered herself a member of the elite, so he had been raised with good manners like I had. Before he died, his father had lost his job and had turned to alcohol, like my foster father.

It was more than background, however. Pierre was intelligent, generous and open-minded. He was a great believer in equality, including the equality of women, and he always showed me respect. He was very proud of me, too—he kept telling his friends how good I was, my accomplishments, my academic career, and all my good qualities. I never really considered myself intelligent in the broad sense of the word—maybe clever and a hard worker—so it made me feel shy and embarrassed to hear so much praise.

So we understood each other very well. However, he did have a fiancée at the time, and we accepted that we were not able to have a romantic relationship. His fiancée was moving to Vancouver, and Pierre was going to do his Masters in urban planning there.

We finished our Mandarin course together. Pierre, having completed his military service, left for Vancouver. He sent me letters regularly. Then, a few months later, he called me at the Saint Denis residence. He said he was feeling emotionally lost. He missed me, he loved me, and he wanted to see me when he came back to France for Christmas.

I told him that I wouldn't start a relationship with him if he was still with his fiancée. He would have to talk about it with her and decide.

He broke up with her, and came to France to see me.

#

At first, I refused to see him. I wasn't convinced that the old relationship was really history. But he slipped a long letter of explanation under the door of my room and said that he would wait outside until he could see me. After a few hours, I peeked out the corridor window. Pierre was still there, patiently waiting in the Christmas cold. I felt guilty and agreed to hear what he had to say. He insisted that he wanted to stay in France, even if it meant quitting his degree.

His mother cautioned him against this, and I agreed with her. It was cheap to study in France, but that wasn't so in Vancouver, and Pierre had already paid for a degree that he was very invested in. He had only one year to go. If he stopped now, he would be throwing away a lot of time and money.

In the end, we decided the best idea would for me to go to Vancouver. We wanted to be together, of course, but I found reason too why Vancouver would be good for my education. Living there would help me learn English. Scientific journals are mainly written in English, so the more I knew, the easier it would be for me to study. Pierre helped me as to enroll in an English intensive course at his school, the University of British Columbia.

For the first few weeks, I stayed with a Canadian host. This is a normal part of an English program. The student gets constant practice in the new language, as well as exposure to the customs and culture of the country. In return, the host receives money from the university.

But the woman I stayed with lived alone and was frequently out. Her son came over some time, but didn't talk to me much, preferring to watch TV. The commute to the university was long, and my bedroom was in the basement, which was getting cold and damp as winter came on. I called Pierre sometimes to complain. I began to feel dispirited about the situation. Soon we moved together into a small, two-person flat at the university campus.

#

At the time I arrived in Vancouver, I had been trying for two or three years to get approved for French naturalization, because I was still considered a political refugee. French citizenship would be a great help, making it easier to get a job and to travel, even back to Cambodia. At the time, there were lots of refugees and foreigners moving to France, which was stirring up nationalist sentiments among some people to close the doors. I would feel much safer if I could hurry up and get citizenship.

Before my break with my French mother, she had asked if I wanted her to officially adopt me. This would have given me automatic French citizenship. It would also have given me the same rights to inherit as her other children had. However, the idea of planning to get someone's possessions when they died was morbid to me. And in any case I thought I'd have an easy time getting naturalization on my own. Surely I was the ideal candidate: I had lived in the country for 15 years, attended school in France, ate French food, spoke the language fluently, and studied at a French university. I was single and wouldn't request to have any relatives naturalized with me. I could barely remember my childhood in Cambodia. I couldn't even speak my mother tongue.

However, French officials had rejected my application. The only reason they gave was that I "had to be integrated professionally." At the time I applied, I had just finished my diploma. How could they expect me to have a job right away? This seemed unfair. I knew people who had gotten citizenship but had never studied in France, didn't speak French, and sometimes were on French welfare.

So while I was in Vancouver in 1997, I decided I would pay a lawyer to follow up and file an appeal. After a few months, she told me that it was no use—my appeal had been rejected.

I was very disappointed. I began to see a gap between the French motto, "Liberty, Equality and Fraternity," and the way that the country's officials treated refugees. Twice now I had been rejected by a country whose ideals I respected so much. It felt like no matter how hard I worked, how loyal I was, or what I could contribute to society, administrative officials saw me as just another piece of paper to stamp—or not. They didn't see the human before them.

#

All the time while I was studying in Vancouver, I couldn't stop thinking about Cambodia. It desperately needed rebuilding. I began to promise myself that I would give something back to my native country—a full year of my life, in fact. I would work in Cambodia for that period of time in some development-oriented job. After the palm reading, that prediction that I would die young still haunted me. I felt like I had to move ahead while there was still time.

Pierre thought this was a great idea. On the Christmas holiday just before he finished his Masters, we spent many hours in his office, until very late at night, looking for jobs or volunteer positions in Southeast Asia.

After days searching on the Internet, sending application after application by fax, e-mail and post, I found the Institut Pasteur in Ho Chi Minh City in Vietnam, and then the Institut Pasteur in Cambodia (IPC). I knew I shouldn't go back to Cambodia while I was still considered a political refugee, but I supposed it wouldn't hurt to send just one more letter.

To my surprise, several days later, I got an e-mail reply. Subject: "Your Job Offer"! It was a laboratory supervisor job, with the grand salary of US$150 per month.

I said yes.

-8-
A Year in -and for- Cambodia

When I told Nguon that I was going to move back to Cambodia, I thought he would be happy. After all, he was always insisting that I should be a typical Cambodian girl. But he wasn't happy at all. He actually did his best to discourage me, insisting that the very tense political situation made life there too dangerous. He actually said I'd end up getting shot dead on the street like a dog.

After the Khmer Rouge, a civil war had broken out in Cambodia between rival factions. It raged for more than a decade, ending only in 1991 with a peace agreement under by which the United Nations would help the country work to become a democracy. All sides swore off further external interference in Cambodian politics. The Cambodian people would determine their own destiny.

The UN sent a large force of peacekeepers who oversaw a national election in 1993. Ninety percent of Cambodia's registered voters cast ballots—a turnout of 4.2 million people. The UN declared that the election had been "fair and free." In September 1993, a new government took office, with two prime ministers, Prince Norodom Ranariddh of the royalist FUNCINPEC party, and Hun Sen of the Cambodian People's Party (CPP).

The two men remained in conflict with each other, despite technically co-running the country. Both of them were trying to convince the last of the Khmer Rouge members to defect to their parties. Finally, on July 5, 1997, the CPP-loyal military confronted the FUNCINPEC. Fighting lasted for 36 hours in Phnom Penh and other places. At the end of it, Prime Minister Ranariddh and many of his high-ranking aides fled to the Thai border, splitting the FUNCINPEC party. They were replaced by members who were loyal to the CPP.

On July 26, 1998, Cambodia conducted a second national election. The CPP was the official winner against FUNCINPEC and the Sam Rainsy Party, but those parties claimed electoral fraud. The CPP controlled the committee overseeing the election, the parties noted, and also much of the radio and television broadcasting leading up to the vote. There were reports of intimidation by the CPP, particularly targeting the poorer and less-educated sections of Cambodian society. In Phnom Penh, the atmosphere remained tense after the vote. A curfew was in place, and violence often erupted.

It is easy to see why Nguon didn't want me to go back. He saw that I had had a great privilege in being able to escape to the developed world. Returning to Cambodia at this time seemed to him like suicide.

However, I brushed aside his pleas. Since reuniting with my family, I had become aware of the injustices occurring in Cambodia, and how much reconstruction the country needed after the Khmer Rouge. I can honestly say that it didn't matter that I might be risking my life: I was determined to help. I was young and wanted to keep my promise to myself.

#

It was very important to me that, once I moved back to Cambodia, I would not depend on my family. Since I was from a developed country, I should help them, not the other way around. The IPC job didn't pay much, but since it was only for a year, I decided that I could make things work. Pierre, however, hadn't yet found a job, so we decided that I would go to Cambodia and get settled, and he would join me three months later. I informed IPC of my refugee status, and that I would enter the country with my French travel documents, which mentioned my status. It was a risk—if I got in trouble, the French Embassy could do nothing to protect me.

I arrived in Phnom Penh in September 1998, more than 18 years after the day I left Cambodia on a truck as a child refugee. Chhay was waiting at the airport to welcome me.

I met my family again, and after that, one of my wishes was to see our former village in Kampong Phnom, 50 kilometers outside of the city. One weekend, I set out for it with Chhay on the back of his motorbike. After we left Phnom Penh, Chhay said he wanted me to learn to drive his bike. He gave a very brief explanation of the basic parts and controls. Then I put it into practice while he took the back seat and helped me balance. I was doing fine driving slowly, but then he instructed me to shift the foot-pedal from speed one to speed two and accelerate. Suddenly we took off. I was surprised by the speed and lost control. We finished on the side of the road in the grass. That was the first and last time I drove a motorbike!

With Chhay again as driver, we arrived safely at our village. I was excited and at the same time nostalgic to see again the place of my childhood memory.

When I saw it, I barely recognized it. It seemed like a desert, devoid of life, with none of the cries of playing children that I remembered. The change extended even to the river with the huge water hyacinths where during the Khmer Rouge time I had almost drowned. Now the river was dried out and the wooden bridge from which I had fallen had disappeared. All that remained was a shallow curve of the river bed. Here and there in the middle some wild water spinach grew, intermixed with wild grass and offal.

Things seemed so small and odd compared to my childhood recollection. I was disappointed and disenchanted to not encounter the scenery engraved in my childhood memory. I felt nostalgic and sad as if the small girl of those times was dead and her childhood had vanished too!

Maybe this had been the meaning of the palm reading that I would "die young." It was like I had had multiple lives and childhoods, an early one in Cambodia and another in France. An odd sensation was slowly rising up from my guts and clouding my mind. Then Chhay called to me and I snapped out of it.

We got on the road again to the nearby town of Neak Loeung to meet two uncles from my father's side and other relatives who survived the Khmer Rouge or were born after their fall from power. I had not yet picked up the Khmer language but I could sense that they were enchanted to see the young woman I had become. They recalled the last time they saw me, how small I was! Still they could recognize family traits such as my eyes, my nose and smile. Overall, the consensus was, I looked like my sister Heang. Now I was back, and in my relatives' eyes it was unbelievable that I would be working with French expats at IPC, the most expert health workers in Cambodia. As a laboratory manager at IPC, I was a great pride for the family, an outstanding niece who was back to our roots helping to build up our country.

I didn't know it that day, but another part of my restored Cambodian identity would soon fall into place—a Cambodian passport, obtained with the help of IPC.

For my first three months in Phnom Penh, I slept in a room at the institute, because there was a curfew. It was too dangerous to go out for no good reason. The institute was located near the French Embassy on one of the city's main streets, Preah Monivong Boulevard. On that same street were the Calmette hospital, the FUNCINPEC office, the University of Health, the Ministry of Communication, and several other important offices, so this was one of the main locations for political demonstrations. Like me, most of IPC's French expatriates were living inside the compound at this time, waiting for security updates from the French embassy.

After three months, the political tensions had abated. There were only small street demonstrations. It was becoming safe to move around the city, and the IPC told me that it could no longer give me the special favor of accommodation. So I moved to a small, dark and rather dirty room in the Chba Ampoev district, near the flat where Ma and Chhay's family lived. We would take our meals all together, except during the working day when I would eat lunch at IPC with my colleagues.

Lots of food vendors were always doing business at Calmette hospital, IPC's immediate neighbor to the rear. We could order delicious meals at almost any time of the day for a very good price. Food and money were exchanged through the metal bars of a fence dividing the two institutions. In the morning around 10 am, my colleagues and I would meet up for tasty breakfast soup. I often ordered one of two kinds: kuyteav, my favorite from Saigon refugee days, or nom banh chok samlor Khmer, with cold rice noodles topped with warm fish gravy and raw greens such as cucumbers, banana blossom, water hyacinth flowers, and water lily stems. With fresh herbs sprinkled on top, everything came together as a soup that smelled yummy! One down side was that these soups were sold in plastic bags. At that time in Cambodia, use of the bags was proliferating out of control, creating a growing environmental problem. In Phnom Penh, plastic bags clogged drainage systems, worsening flooding during the rainy season. It was just another problem compounding the health issues Cambodia was already facing.

The rent at my new home was $50 per month. I hired a motorbike and driver—called a motodoub in Cambodia—to take me to and from work for $20 per month. Instead of taxis or cars, the common transport in Phnom Penh was the motodoub or cyclobike, a sort of pedal rickshaw. The roads were mostly dirt and very rough and bumpy.

#

Every day I was reminded how living in Cambodia was different than living in France. Blackouts were so frequent that all households had candles for backup lights, and the IPC had a backup generator. Electrical appliances like fridges and freezers were rare, except among expats and foreign institutions. Cambodian locals used ice boxes.

Local people got up with the early morning light just as the roosters started to crow, and rushed to the markets to buy food. There was only one supermarket in the city of about a million people. It had very expensive imported goods, but even the local goods were costly. So most people just went to the local markets, even though they were crowded and muddy.

The political situation was reasonably stable now, but I still needed to be vigilant against pickpockets in the open-air markets. On my first morning at the Chba Ampoev market with my sister-in-law, Saor, Chhay's wife, I brought my large, navy blue Eastpak satchel. It was empty, but I had it with me to carry anything I bought and my Cambodian passport, which I would need to change money. Saor led me to an exchange shack, where I turned over a $100 bill and got back nearly half a million riels, Cambodia's currency.

We moved on. In one of the busy alleys, I was pushed from behind a little, but I couldn't move forward because someone was directly in front of me.

Suddenly, one of the vendors screamed, "Thief! Thief!"

Still very agitated, she told Saor that she had seen someone try to open my bag with a razor blade from behind. The thief had had a helper, who was preventing me from moving forward by pretending to browse in front of me. For a moment, I panicked. Saor told me to check my bag, quickly. Thankfully, it had multiple compartments, and my money and passport were still in the inner pocket. There didn't appear to be any holes in the bag, either. Saor and I continued with our errands.

It wasn't until Monday morning at the IPC office that I opened my Eastpak to get my books and documents out and saw the huge slash. It was about fifteen centimeters long. I shivered just thinking of the razor blade swiping so close to me! But I also felt very lucky that I hadn't lost any money or my passport.

One weekend, early in the morning, I heard a sudden scream, followed by panicked voices from downstairs in Chhay's house. Shortly after, Chhay knocked on my room door and entered with intense fear on his face. He asked me to come downstairs quickly to help Ma. She had fallen in the wet bathroom and split open her head! Everyone in the house was frightened seeing the blood coming out and wetting her grey hair. Ma was silent, sitting half conscious. I was not sure of what to do either but in Fontainebleau I had taken a basic life-saving class with the firefighters and one important thing I knew was to keep calm and assess the situation. I cleaned up her wound and shaved the hair around it to have a better look. Fortunately it was not too bad; it was just a big bump and a shallow cut. I applied the antiseptic wound solution Betadine and a bandage. My family members saw me as a savior, for keeping calm and for not being afraid to look at the bloody scene. Everyone felt better and the tension waned. Later, we made gentle jokes and laughed that our mother had a kbal rung, which means a hard head and suggests a person is stubborn. Even Ma smiled a little. Long ago, she used to call me a little stubborn girl and now I could say from whom I got my stubbornness!

From that time, Chhay told Ma that whenever she wanted to move around she had to call someone to accompany her, even to the bathroom, as she could barely see.

#

Phnom Penh had one main landfill for the waste that was collected across the city. A large community of very poor families, in fact several villages of them, were living right in the landfill to scavenge for plastic and cans that they could sell for recycling. Even children took part in this hazardous work. When I was living in Phnom Penh, I sometimes collected my old clothes and went to the landfill to give them to the families there. I usually spent only an hour, but even that was enough to impregnate my clothes with the smell of filth. But it seemed an obvious thing to do if I was serious about helping out the destitute.

Poverty and insecurity stared you in the face across Cambodia in those days, but people were nonetheless very pleasant, polite and often had a sense of naïveté. They talked to each other. They could seem almost stoic in the face of having almost no opportunities for work or education or even simple play.

Nowadays, Cambodia has changed drastically. There are rich people—and a big gap between them and the large numbers of poor who remain. Glass high-rises have gone up in Phnom Penh and other cities. People have fridges, so they don't need to visit the local markets on a daily basis. In any case, many prefer to shop in air-conditioned supermarkets. Innovations like the Internet and mobile phones have opened people to new ideas. Yet they have also made people more materialistic and selfish. People are less friendly on the streets. They are busier and don't stop to talk. They are globally connected through the Internet, but they don't trust people living right next door as they did before. Progress has brought Cambodia some good things, but it's not hard to list things you wish had remained unchanged.

#

The IPC had two major divisions: The medical lab and the research lab. In fact, each of these had different laboratories within them—medical had chemistry, bacteriology and parasitology units, and research had virology and molecular biology units. The institute earned income by doing medical tests for hospitals, NGOs and individual patients.

First, I worked in the medical laboratory. My role was to supervise and teach the laboratory team. I made sure that their work habits were standardized, that they wrote down all their analysis procedures, and that they knew how to get accurate results. After a few months, I moved to the research lab division, specifically to HIV functions in the virology unit. I prepared nationwide quality controls for HIV analysis to send to a list of Cambodian medical laboratories. I also taught medical French to the Cambodian employees.

The director and head of my section were both French expatriates. French university trainees were conducting research projects there as well. However, most of the staff I worked with were Cambodians. They were Khmer Rouge survivors older than I. They were all friendly, eager both to learn and to talk about their experiences from Khmer Rouge days. Some of the older staff became like relatives to me. They would bring food or fruit for us all to share. I had to always remind them that it was forbidden to eat in the lab, but I enjoyed it as much as anyone, so I sometimes broke that rule like everyone else. We spent time together outside the IPC as well, going on picnics at their homes in the countryside, and to festivals and celebrations. It was like being the beloved youngest child in a big family. They helped me improve my Khmer, and very soon I was able to communicate in that language both at work and with my Cambodian family. I also hired a Khmer teacher to improve my writing and reading skills in lessons after office hours at the IPC.

In the meantime, Pierre had arrived. He now had his Master's. In late 1998, he found volunteer work in Cambodia with Action Nord Sud, a French NGO that was part of Handicap International. His role was to research, design and implement social development projects in the country's slums. He would earn just enough so that our combined income could support a modest life. Through his work with the NGO, we obtained free accommodation, and I moved out of the tiny apartment I was renting.

After my promotion to the virology unit, I had a salary of $350 per month. I worked for Dominique, a French MD/PhD candidate. She needed time to focus on writing her thesis, so I assisted her through her last few months of lab experiments and research on HIV. My horizons expanded: I learned about immunology and the molecular biology of HIV/AIDS. I learned multiple techniques for diagnosing HIV/AIDS, including the system known as ELISA, nucleic acid extraction, and gene amplification. I learned how to diagnose HIV infection in babies from HIV-positive mothers and to spot the human rabies virus in saliva.

Dominique was very happy with the quality of my lab work, because I gave fast and clean results. I started to read more scientific papers. I really enjoyed the scientific process, the exploration of hypotheses, and the excitement of getting and interpreting lab results.

#

Pierre and I travelled often in this period, to outlying provinces and surrounding countries. We loved discovering new places and new people together.

We went to the north of Cambodia to Ratanak Kiri Province. At the time, it was very difficult to get to. The roads had been destroyed, and it was nearly impossible to go there by car. We had to take a tiny airplane—it was so small it was scary. I felt it could fall out of the sky at any moment.

Once there, we went off the beaten path to meet local people and to get to know their cultures. Their dialect of Khmer was difficult for people from other areas to understand. But the culture was fascinating— their funeral customs, for instance. Rather than mourning a death, they would hold a festival to celebrate the departed, with plenty of food and rice wine and the sacrifice of a cow or buffalo. At the grave, they would place statues to commemorate the dead for who they were. For example, a hunter's grave might be marked by statues of dead animals. Pierre and I walked through the open cemeteries, amazed at these totems.

We hired guides to take us by boat to meet remote tribes. We tried the local rice wine, which was made in a jar. After we had drunk from it through a long bamboo straw, people added more water to the jar, closed it, and let alcohol ferment inside.

We went to Thailand too. There we visited tribes who stretched their ear lobes down to their shoulders. We spent time with others who wore huge ceramic plates in their lips or heavy brass rings around their necks. The rings pushed down on their collar bones, making the women look long-necked, almost like a giraffe.

#

Around December of 1998, Chhay finished building a house of his own in Phnom Penh. Cambodians considered this time of the year to be a short winter season because the temperature can drop for a few days down to 16 or 17 Celsius, which was cold for us when we were used to 35 degrees Celsius as an annual average. During this time of the year, we used our traditional clay cook stoves, filled with glowing charcoal embers, to warm up the house. One morning, Soar and a housekeeper, Srey Neang, put with the kindest of intentions a stove full of embers near Ma's bed to warm her up. But very quickly one of them noticed a smell— it seemed a mixture of singed hair and roasted pork. They turned to see Ma's foot above the charcoal stove and her heel roasting! Her advanced diabetes had prevented Ma from feeling the heat. Luckily the harm to her foot was not too bad.

Early in 1999, Ma's health worsened. She was losing her appetite, even for her favorite foods. Her limbs and feet started to swell until one day she could barely breathe. I was at IPC working when my sister Heang called me and told me they were in an ambulance taking Ma to the Calmette hospital, next door to IPC.

I found them waiting at the emergency room. Ma was in her sarong, lying on a stretcher among other patients. There was an unspoken understanding in Cambodian hospitals that whoever would bribe the employees and doctors would receive care first. Even though I was desperate to get help for Ma, I took the hard decision to ask my family members not to perpetuate the immoral practice of bribery.

They reluctantly complied, but I knew that as a Cambodian daughter I had a duty to do something special to help Ma.

Calmette often sent patient samples to IPC for analysis. We conducted research projects involving its patients and in exchange the patients got free medical analysis. I was rubbing shoulders daily with some of the Cambodian and French doctors involved in this cooperation. So that day, for the first time, I reluctantly used my work relationships for the benefit of our family. I asked the French anesthetist and resuscitation doctor at Calmette, Dr. Christian Rathat, if he would please examine and diagnose my mother. He did, and then things became easy afterwards as Cambodian employees at Calmette considered Ma as a very special patient.

Dr. Rathat also performed a puncture procedure to drain two liters of fluid. After that Ma was able to breathe better and had less pain. We were infinitely grateful to the doctor. Without his skilled intervention, Ma may have died that day in excruciating circumstances.

Afterward, Dr. Rathat asked me to come in his office and he gave a thorough and detailed explanation about Ma's health. He compared her body to an old car with a rusted engine that was breaking down. Her advanced untreated diabetes had induced complications, breaking down all her organs. Her kidneys were no longer working to filter toxins from her blood. Glucose being deposited as crystals in her tiny veins was undermining her vision, sensation, and lung function. One of the options was heavy blood dialysis. This would be a long process which would create complications for Ma and a heavy financial burden on the family. At that time, there was only one dialysis center in the country and it belonged to Calmette hospital.

Dr. Rathat suggested instead that we treat her anemia with injections of the Erythropoietin (EPO) growth factor hormone, which would boost production of her red blood cells. His other suggestion—a strong recommendation, really—was for us to take her home, pamper her with whatever she wanted, and make her last days as happy as possible.

Ma stayed a few days at the hospital, sharing the room with four to six other patients. Sadly one roommate died during that short stay. Our family did a continuous relay day and night to be at her bedside and provide her food. Then we took her home and shared responsibility for all the necessary tasks. I was the one who followed up her medical record, gave her EPO injections and withdrew blood samples to analyze at IPC.

We decided to let her resume one of her favorite activities—chewing tobacco. She would make a small ball about a centimeter and a half in diameter, pop it into her mouth and hold it there between lip and teeth. From time to time she spat out saliva. It was a modern version of an ancient Cambodian tradition, the chewing of betel nut. I remember that in pre-war days my grandmother and Ma kept near the sleeping mat a wooden lacquer box which contained all the ingredients to make a daily betel "quid." Women liked to chew a quid as they worked. It would stimulate saliva flow, and, they say, their energy. I can still see Ma sitting on the wooden floor, delicately preparing her quid by coating a green betel leaf with a thin layer of pink slaked lime, then placing in the middle a chunk of betel nut and sprinkling on top a bite of tobacco. Into the mouth it would go. She would spit out the juicy black saliva continuously on the ground. Her smile showed her betel red black teeth!

Nguon and Sophy, still living in Paris, took an early summer holiday to visit us and spend time with Ma. Early on the morning of June 12, 1999, Ma awoke and asked for keatuiv, one of her favorite soups. Then she fell back asleep, and did not reawaken. She was gone.

I was not there, however. I was in Bangkok, tending to Pierre, who was receiving hospital treatment for a severe fever and infection. By the time I got back to Phnom Penh, Chhay and Nguon had had their heads shaved, as the rituals of a Chinese funeral require. I looked at video and photos taken by my family as a record of Ma's death.

The death was sad for us who remained, but for Ma it was relief from what had become a very painful existence. We had all known her end was near. We had done what we could to let her leave this world in peace. In her final days, she was able to see all her remaining children and their children as well.

I and other family members attended funeral rites to mark the seventh day and the hundredth day since Ma's death. The whole experience made me reflect on my hopes that my own death will be quick, not long and excruciating in a hospital. I've often told my family that I don't want elaborate funeral rites when I'm gone. It should be something small, intimate and personal. Just a simple cremation without fancy religious ceremonies will do.

#

My work at IPC was meant to last just a year, but it was extended. By the time I'd been there, I was feeling more and more patriotic. I started to feel a genuine part of the nation of my roots. My Cambodian heritage was reawakening within me. I felt a sense of belonging that I had lost for years. Now I wanted to see the country develop and see Cambodians achieve their potential. I felt I could make my best contribution through medicine. That meant I needed to pursue education at a higher level.

1964: At our village, Kampong Phnom. Pa (on the right carrying a tray) at one of his younger brothers' wedding. On the left, my older brothers Ngoun (1), Khoung (2), and Heng (3).

Early 1981 in Saigon. *Me with my oldest sister who came from Cambodia to visit us.*

Me with Pou family: *Mamie and Miss. Pol.*

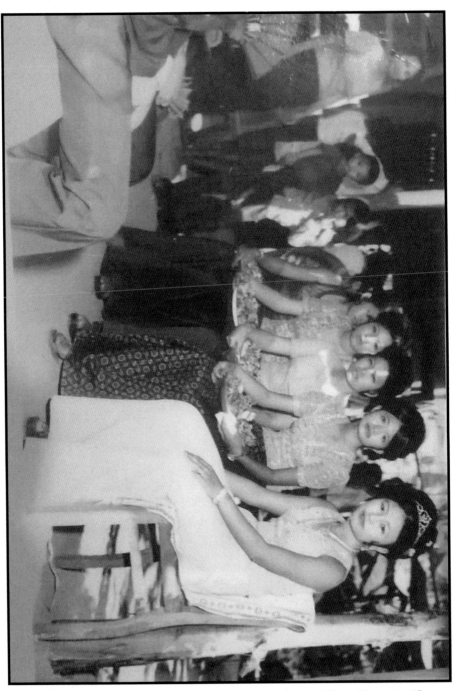

My sister Heang was married in March 1982, in my home village Kampong Phnom.
Here she waits in front of the house with her bridesmaids for the arrival of guests. Ma is in
the back in front of the stairs. I was a schoolgirl living with my French family at the time
and knew nothing of the wedding.

My French family, in late 1981 or early 1982 in Roissy en Brie, a Paris suburb. Front row, from left: Ludovic (in white shirt); Aude a cousin; me; Eric. Middle row: Jean-François; Grandmother "Bonne-manan" of my mother's side; my mother "Maman;" Grandmother "Mamie" of my father's side. Back row: Grandfather "Papy" of my mother's side; Grandfather of my father's side; my father "Papa."

Reunion with my biological family, summer 1995, in Ho Chi Minh City, Vietnam. *At front center is Ma, with Seav Houng on the left and Chou on the right. The baby behind Seav Houng is Lucky; above Chou is Huot. In the back row are, from left, Nguon; Sophy; Chhay; Sor; older sister Eang; me; Heang; Kry Heang's husband; Maeve; and Sokyou.*

—Part Four—

Becoming a Scientist -and Athlete

-9-
Hitting the Books to Earn a PhD

I applied for a Fulbright scholarship at the US Embassy in Phnom Penh to do a Masters in biology in the United States. I only made it through the first round of the selection process. The embassy told me that its priorities for Cambodian awards were economics, business and tourism. Since I wanted to undertake a degree in science, they couldn't offer me a full scholarship. But without a full scholarship I wasn't going to be able to go at all.

At the same time, Pierre had applied in France for a Fulbright fellowship to study in the United States. He got it; he was also accepted to a PhD program at the Massachusetts Institute of Technology (MIT). He was going to move away from Cambodia, though keeping a strong link to it. He would be studying urban poverty on a schedule that would have him spending six months a year in the United States, and six months in Phnom Penh to continue working on poverty reduction. I was happy for him, and proud, but at the same time, I didn't want him to go. I loved Pierre, and I wanted us to stay together. We had built a strong relationship; we were practically a married couple. We inspired each other to work to make a difference and improve the world.

On the other hand Pierre was being offered a tremendous opportunity. Reason won out over emotions, and I didn't beg Pierre to stay. Instead I looked forward to the future, telling myself we could be together after we finished our studies.

\#

Pierre and I talked over the problem of my own scholarship. One of my main concerns was that my training was quite different from what most applicants to a PhD program had. In Paris I had gone through a two-year practical curriculum to be a laboratory assistant while I struggled to make a living on the side. My marks were far from stellar, and I did not have the strong theoretical background and ability to deal with concepts that come from completing a mainstream university curriculum. To obtain a scholarship, I would have to compete with many brilliant students who could be seen as safer choices than I.

We decided I might have a better chance of getting a scholarship to study in the United States if I could raise my score on the TOEFL and GRE exams.

I had already taken the exams in Cambodia, when they were still administered on paper. In the meantime, the tests had gone electronic. There wasn't a facility for that in Cambodia, so in 1999 I went to a test center in Bangkok. Nowadays, there are special schools and tutors who help students with the test, but back then I had to study all on my own. As hard as I tried, I did not get a score that would get me into the universities that I wanted.

At the end of that year, there was a change in direction at IPC. Dr. François Flye Saint Marie, the director, was retiring. Prof. Yves Buisson was to be appointed, in the presence of Prof. Jean Luc Durosoir, director general of the global network of Pasteur Institutes. The IPC staff was all invited to attend the ceremony on the Mekong River's Silk Island near Phnom Penh.

Prior to boarding a boat for the island, Prof. Durosoir came to me and said gently and discreetly that, after the celebration he would like to talk to me, so we should be on the same boat coming back. I was quite surprised. Why would the director general want to talk with me? I wondered if I had done something wrong, but I couldn't think of anything so bad that a man of his rank would want to talk to me about it!

Nervously, Pierre and I got onto the same boat as Prof. Durosoir on the way back. However, I was soon pleasantly surprised and humbled! Instead of telling me that I was in trouble, he said he had heard from the IPC administration that I was applying for a scholarship to study in the United States. He suggested instead that I should pursue my study in the French system, with the Institut Pasteur in Paris and Phnom Penh. But because I had not completed full-length Bachelor's and Master's degrees, the usual preparations for a PhD in France, I would first have to take two graduate courses at IP Paris and write a short thesis regarding my research projects at IP Cambodia. Meanwhile, I'd continue to work with Cambodian patients as my fieldwork. Then I would have a Masters-equivalent degree, and I could enroll in a PhD program. Prof. Durosoir said that he saw me as the locomotive of a train driving progress in Cambodian research.

Despite his praise, his proposal wasn't what I'd wanted. I wouldn't live in the United States and I wouldn't be able to stay with Pierre. But it would let me get my PhD, and my tuition would be free, since I would be working for the Institut while I studied.

We both knew that Pierre studying in the United States and me in France and Cambodia was the best thing for both of us. So we made a pact: We would stay in touch every day while we were apart and take every opportunity to see each other.

#

By now, Pierre and I had decided that we wanted to start a family after we'd done our PhDs. We would need a place to raise our children. I proposed we buy some land in Cambodia and build a house on it. At first, Pierre disagreed. He travelled a lot for work, and so he didn't think it was a good idea to buy land. Besides, from his work with the urban poor and housing rights, he knew how easy it was for the government to seize land and expel its occupants. He did not want to risk all our savings on something that could be taken away from us overnight. But I insisted. I wanted us to have something to call our own.

Pierre relented in the end. After all, the savings we had were mostly my savings, so it was my choice, he said.

I bought a plot near Phnom Penh Thmey, about six kilometers from the center of Phnom Penh. It was quite a nice area, but almost immediately after I bought, the International University started to construct two big buildings there. Within days, the land around mine was all sold. It quickly became clear that this wasn't going to be a peaceful place to raise children.

Luckily, one of the side effects of the development was to drive land prices up. So I sold my plot for a profit and bought another, further away from the bustle of development.

This was where we started to build our house. Pierre and I agreed that it should be as close to a traditional Cambodian house as possible. It should be eco-friendly, not needing much air conditioning or power. That meant a high roof for good air circulation and big, sliding windows. We wanted to make it out of traditional, local materials, that is, lots of wood. As we had travelled together, we had often collected ideas for what we would incorporate into our house. We wanted three bedrooms, so that we would have room for the children, and an office or study room, so that Pierre could run a consulting business from home.

For the design, we hired a local architect. There weren't many architects in Cambodia at the time, but we were very happy with ours. He discussed the design with us, told us a lot about the local materials we would be working with, and helped us figure out what would and wouldn't work. He warned us, for example, that the Cambodian tile we had planned wouldn't be as durable as traditional Vietnamese tile. He was very understanding of our requirements. We eventually settled on a design and he began to direct the work.

#

I flew off to Paris and began work toward my PhD. My thesis would build on my work in Cambodia: It would create the first database on the effects that antiretrovirals, newly introduced drugs for treating HIV, were having on patients in the country.

I found myself rubbing shoulders with some of the great professors of medicine. I felt so small. I was so impressed by them—I had so much to learn!

For instance, Prof. Françoise Barré-Sinoussi taught our class on the HIV virus. Later on, in 2008 she received the Nobel Prize for the actual discovery of the virus.

We students all respected her. She dressed very elegantly, and although she could come across as a bit cold and distant, she was going to be my PhD scientific advisor.

One day early on, she started a class by telling me that she wanted to see me in her office afterwards, I was so anxious that all I could say was "Yes! Yes!"

Through the whole class, I was worried about why I was being called to the office, just like when Prof. Durosoir asked me to meet him on the boat. During a break in the class, a friend of mine started to make jokes about it, and the classmates joined in, calling me a VIP, to have a private meeting with such an important person!

Again, just like with Prof. Durosoir, I was pleasantly surprised. Prof. Barré-Sinoussi had been part of the decision to let me study at the Institut Pasteur. She said that the board was very interested in developing scientific leaders in Cambodia, and they all wanted me to succeed. She took me to dinner to meet other well known professors, such as Prof. Hervé Fleury, who was a PH-PU—that is, he had positions both as a professor at a public hospital, and a university professor. Prof. Fleury would be my PhD mentor. The current manager of the IPC Virology Department, Dr. Jean Marc Reynes, would be my lab mentor.

The next time I went to class, my classmates interrogated me about the meeting. This was another pleasant surprise. Most of the other students had come to this course directly from their university studies, whereas I had been working in the field for few years. I hadn't read as many academic reports as they had, and I didn't know a lot of the things that they had studied. But, when they included me in their joking like that, they seemed to consider me as one of them. I felt happy to be their equal, despite my different background.

I promised myself that I would concentrate on my thesis and do well in my studies. I knew I was very lucky to be studying where I was, with free tuition. The only way I had of repaying those who had faith in me was to work hard and succeed. I felt like the Chosen One! They were all putting in such effort to guide me, and advocate for me to represent Cambodia as a scientist, to help rebuild the nation. I was enchanted to have Prof. Barré-Sinoussi as my scientific supervisor. She was not at all cold once you got to know her. She even liked me to call her by her first name, Françoise.

Prof. Durosoir also requested me to visit him at his office. In subsequent months, he frequently checked if I was doing well during the course. He told me my success was important. He said that if I ever had any troubles, I knew where to find him, and he would help—even talk to other professors on my behalf if there was trouble.

One significant problem I had was that my practical rather than academic background made the academic reading more difficult. Everyone spoke French in class, but the readings were in academic English. It's much more difficult than conversational English. I could make my way through most of the papers, but I often had to spend late nights and weekends doing extra reading, searching on the Internet, and reading papers over again to understand the scientific jargon. On this issue, I felt a huge gap with some of the other students.

Thankfully, our class had a collaborative atmosphere. While most students were from university backgrounds, a few had been lab technicians and supervisors like me in the IP network. We all combined our skills and helped each other out. There was no sense of competition—we weren't fighting for jobs. All in all, I felt very cared for and fortunate. I swore to myself that I would make the professors proud and prove their choice right, so the IP would later grant a similar chance to others like me.

Sometimes, when I got a few minutes' break in the daily rush of tasks, I dared to look down the road a few years. I saw myself at the helm of an advanced Institut Pasteur laboratory in Cambodia, conducting original research on infectious diseases. Who could say, but this lab and its team might make major discoveries that would improve public health in Cambodia and other countries. I naively dreamed of winning a Nobel Prize. I knew how unlikely that was, but I knew also that when it did happen, it was the result of the kind of hard work that I was determined to apply.

#

December 04th, 2002, Pierre asked me to marry him.

He expected me to jump with joy. For him, getting married was a huge milestone. Not for me. Being married would not really be any different from what we already had. In Cambodia, it was considered unusual, and a bit unseemly, for a man and a woman to live together if they weren't married, so we already referred to each other as "my husband" and "my wife" when we were in public. I already respected and loved Pierre, and I already planned to spend my life supporting him. In my eyes, we were already a committed couple. A wedding would just be a formality.

Maybe I would have been more excited if it meant we'd be living under the same roof, not heading to different continents after the ceremony. So I said, "Yeah, if you want to and if you do the paperwork." I think my subdued response surprised him a little, but he agreed.

Pierre asked his best friend, an Australian named Peter who was working in Phnom Penh, to be a witness, and I asked my sister-in-law. We signed our marriage documents at the Tonle Bassac district office and notified the French Embassy. That evening, the four of us went for a nice dinner. There was to be no honeymoon—we would wait for later, after a celebration for our family and friends, and when we had the money.

I had expected Pierre to ask me to take his family name, but when he handed me documents that would register our marriage with the French Embassy, I could see he had written in "Nary Ly," my name just as it was.

I asked him why, and he told me that he hadn't wanted to pressure me or assume anything. He would be more than happy for me to change my name if I wanted, but he hadn't thought it was right to force it on me.

In the end, I kept my last name "Ly." But this was part of why I loved Pierre so much. He was thoughtful enough not only to consider the question, but to let me decide. Later his mother too seemed surprised by his very culturally unusual attitude towards me.

#

I was usually the one who supervised the house construction. Pierre was in the United States basically all the time, but I was in Cambodia at least some of the time, in between courses in Paris at IP learning specific lab techniques and in Bordeaux at the University Hospital.

While I really wanted the house, and spent a lot of time supervising construction that seemed never to end, I was becoming exhausted trying to keep up on so many different fronts—work, study, construction. I just wanted the house to be finished. At the same time, I wanted the job to be done well as we would only get one chance to build.

All IPC staff got a two-hour lunch break, so I would go and see the construction site then, and on the weekends too. If I didn't go there, I went to the gym or practiced a Korean martial art with North Korean instructors. I learned the history, the moral codes, the manner of each stance of the version of the art practiced by the International Taekwon-Do Federation. Over the course of training, I had three different North Korean instructors, who succeeded each other based on the time they were allowed to stay in Cambodia. We became good friends. Many times, my instructors strongly encouraged me to take part in competitions.

They saw in me a great chance to win in my category, light-weight. But I refused their offers, because I didn't like to fight with an opponent.

What I liked was that Tae Kwon-do kept me healthy and fit.

The house took two years to finish. I lived in it from 2005 onwards.

#

In 2003, Pierre received a job offer to work at the World Bank, in their Young Professionals Program. We knew it could open the way to lifelong employment in one of the most influential development aid agencies. By then, he had been working on his PhD for more than two years. He decided to take the offer and try continuing his studies while working full-time. He could always leave after a couple of years if the double burden did not work out.

I went to visit Pierre several times during his job with the World Bank. His first assignment was at its headquarters in Washington, DC. I had to get a G2 spouse's visa to enter the United States and a special badge to pass through the doors of the bank's very well secured building. If I'd wanted, the visa would have let me work in America.

His World Bank colleagues were all quite surprised that I was staying in Cambodia while he worked in Washington. They didn't understand why I would keep on in a developing country when I could live in comfort with Pierre. But Pierre was proud of me and what I was working for, and he told them that I was a very independent woman, who didn't want to take advantage of him. We both wanted to succeed on our own, and we supported each other's choices.

#

While I was finishing my PhD, my lab mentor Dr. Reynes was moved to another Institute Pasteur, in Madagascar. At IP Paris, there were also big changes in the hierarchy. The position of director general of the Pasteur Network was eliminated just a year after Prof. Durosoir retired. The head of Paris IP would now also manage the global network of 33 institutes and affiliates. There were local changes, too. Dr. Reynes had been the sole manager of the virology unit. When he left, he was replaced by two managers. This re-organization sparked tension between these two regarding their responsibilities, lab space and staff numbers. In the end, the virology unit was split into two labs. One manager was responsible for HIV and hepatitis viruses, and the other managed influenza, dengue, rabies and the remaining viruses.

This all had impact on my situation. Paris headquarters no longer had Prof. Durosoir's commitment to build a Cambodian scientist corps. It seemed that what was going on in France was all that mattered to the organization. The branches in other countries were there to serve headquarters. I started to see this reality and felt disappointed that local scientists' work and ideas were no longer a priority. It didn't seem to matter to the Paris leadership that we were constantly thrown into disarray. I felt like we were now considered cheap labor.

#

Finally, finally, the day drew near on which I would complete my PhD. The last step, scheduled for October 2006, would be to present my thesis at the University of Bordeaux.

I wanted to do something personal to mark this milestone, so I invited my foster parents and Pierre and his mother. Communication with my foster parents had been very limited in recent years, and at times I was uncertain about their feelings towards me. However, to thank them for taking me in for those nine years, I bought their train tickets and paid for their hotel rooms and all their meals. I really wanted to honor them for their contribution to my life.

Even though I had spent so much time preparing my presentation, rehearsing it over and over again, on the day itself I felt emotional turbulence. I would have only 45 minutes to detail three years of work with a PowerPoint presentation, and to answer all the questions from the jury.

The jurors and my friends and relatives made their way into the examination room while I sat at its center, waiting for my turn to start. Everyone was staring at me. I was so tense. My hands were cold. Then the president of the jury asked everyone to stand for the introduction of the jury members. Then, he said, would come the subject of the day: defense of a PhD by Nary Ly.

Once I was told to start, I took a deep breath and knew I would be fine. I spoke clearly. My PowerPoint was good—plenty of colorful illustrations and animations to make the subject easy to understand. I felt energized and absorbed in my demonstration, sharing my exciting results with the jury. I was in harmony. I was the maestro! I felt I answered the jury's questions perfectly.

After my defense, we all had to leave the room for five or ten minutes to let the jury discuss my research and presentation. While we waited, various people told me they thought I gave an excellent defense. It was good to hear that, but I needed the jury's confirmation.

When we were called back to the room, I stood silently to hear their answer. In one of my life's greatest moments of joy and pride, they awarded me a High Distinction for my PhD! I was thrilled and thankful. What a wonderful day it was—and what a happy ending to the long and arduous PhD process.

After that, we all went to the Bordeaux 2 university lab, where my Bordeaux friends and colleagues joined us for a cocktail party.

While we were getting our drinks, maman surprised me. She gave a brief speech to the professors there, and for the first time I could remember, I heard her say that she was proud of me and my accomplishments. She explained with tears in her eyes that she has her own four children and they all received the same amount of love and education, yet I was the only child who had achieved so much. It gave me deep satisfaction to hear her say these things. At last, I had my parents' trust and pride, and they considered me a mature woman.

Then my colleagues had some surprises for me. They had written a song for me and they distributed copies around the room, so everyone could sing in chorus! I stood there listening to many blush-worthy lines, set to the tune of the popular French song *"Petite Marie"* (Little Marie). I was "little fury" who was "looking for paradise in the middle of brambles."

Little Fury, you say that life

Is only worth living if you have a choice

To do what you want,

Surrounded by people who support you.

It was a warm and amazing atmosphere. I got gifts, letters, and gift cards full of kind messages. I was very moved.

Afterwards, I treated my foster parents, Pierre, his mother and a scientist friend Francis to a nice dinner in the center of Bordeaux.

That was the last time I ever saw my foster father. He passed away a year later, in December 2007. But the reunion in Bordeaux marked the start of a reconciliation with maman that would give me deep joy and satisfaction in the years to come.

#

In my final months at Bordeaux, I became aware of an upcoming set of races in Cambodia that would raise money for care of HIV patients. It was the Angkor Wat International Half Marathon, in which runners race among the great sandstone temples of the civilization that flourished in Cambodia in ancient times. It also included a 10K event. I wanted to do something new to mark the end of my studies. So I decided I would run the 10K.

I had no idea that this decision would lead to a whole new passion in my life.

I had run before, as part of sports—the warm-up in Tae Kwondo, for instance. But I never focused on it. Now I knew I would need some kind of training. So I began running at the university stadium during my lunch break, counting my laps on the 400-meter track. Every day or so, I tried to increase the number of laps, pushing myself a bit harder. Sometimes, co-workers joined me, and we shared some enjoyable times. I remember changing into my sports clothes between shelves in the virology library, where I worked on my thesis.

I didn't have proper equipment for running, so for my PhD graduation, I asked for some running gear as gifts. My sister-in-law Sophy gave me Nike shoes and a running top. At the time, Nike and Apple had a collaboration, and the shoes had a hole in them where you could put a running sensor. Pierre bought me a first-generation iPod with a running sensor to go with the shoes. On the back of the iPod, he had the words "Free Spirit" engraved for me.

I arrived back in Cambodia and continued to train. I was more motivated than ever with my new gear, and I had much more time now that I was free from my thesis writing. I learned to use the mini iPod with the sensor, and then I went out running on asphalt roads.

One weekend, Pierre accompanied me on his bike for my morning training. I was running from our home in Phnom Penh Thmey to the Monument of Independence in the center of Phnom Penh and back, about 18 kilometers. Afterwards, Pierre said, "Hey, you don't look very tired after 18 kilometers. Why don't you sign up for something longer than just 10?"

So the next day, I went to register for the race at the Olympic stadium in Phnom Penh. I learned that there were only two distances: 10 kilometers or the half marathon—21 kilometers.

I asked for the half marathon. The secretary who was taking my registration was startled. Even though I had handed her my Cambodian ID and was speaking Khmer to her, she looked surprised. "Are you really Cambodian?" she asked with some excitement. "So far we've never had a Cambodian woman run the half." I assured her I was indeed Cambodian, and once she'd accepted that, she asked to keep my contact details for the future. Every year, she told me, Singapore sent two invitations for a half marathon international event, one for a Cambodian woman and one for a Cambodian man. But to date they had never found a female runner to invite.

I agreed, but did some full disclosure: This would be my first time running that distance, and I wasn't sure I would reach the finish line. I was now thinking of doing a post doctorate (postdoc) outside Cambodia, so I might not be available to take part. But I agreed that yes, if I was in Cambodia when the invitation came, I would be honored to represent the country in Singapore.

#

I sent messages to all my friends at the Institut Pasteur network, announcing that I was going to run a half-marathon and asking for donations for the race charities. My overseas friends, including classmates from my course at the Institut Pasteur in Paris, contributed to the cause as well.

However, some of my classmates who knew a bit about running asked, "Are you sure you want to do a half-marathon? Are you certain? Have you trained for it?"

I told them I was in training, and that there was no option between 10K and the half-marathon. I told them I would just have to try my best and hope I crossed the finish line. In the end, I think they felt encouraged to donate a little more, because the race would be such a challenge for me. I raised almost $1,000 for children with HIV.

Looking back now, I realize how naïve I was. I knew nothing about marathons or half marathons when I ran that race. I didn't know how to train, I didn't have a race strategy, I didn't bring anything sugary to refuel myself with during the race. And I thought that if you stopped running and walked, you would be disqualified.

About 2,000 runners turned out that year at the starting line, located in front of the iconic temple Angkor Wat. The gun sounded and off we went. For a while I felt I was doing well, but I didn't know how to pace myself, so by the time I reached the 15th kilometer, I was exhausted. I was out of energy and slowing down. The last few kilometers seemed impossible. I didn't think I'd reach the finish line.

However, I found unexpected support in the form of my 15-year-old niece, Seav Houng, daughter of my brother Chhay. She was spending a few days with me at the time and had come to cheer me on. The race was starting and finishing at the same spot, and I had told her rather firmly that she must remain there and not get lost. But when she saw the joyful crowd take off to cheer runners at different places along the course, she simply couldn't hold herself back. She called a motodoub over, and paid him to catch up with the pack of runners, trying to spot me.

Finally, she saw me at kilometer 15. I was still running, exhausted, but determined not to stop. I still thought I would be disqualified if I fell back to walking, so I was pushing myself as hard as I could to keep running.

Then I heard her calling to me. "Aunty! Aunty!"

It was like waking up. I looked up. The motodoub had pulled up alongside me. Seav Houng was on the back, trying to take photographs of me.

It was wonderful to see her joyful face, bouncing up and down, both with excitement and because the road was bumpy. She was right at my side when I needed her most. Her disobedience was completely forgiven, as she gave me the determination I needed to keep going. Suddenly a wave of energy hit me. I picked my head up and kept running.

One kilometer before the finish line, Seav Houng drove ahead to let Pierre know I was coming, and to prepare to get the best possible pictures of me at the finish line. With a final burst of energy, I crossed it.

Later, I found out that all the pictures Seav Houng took of me in the final stretch were blurry, from the rough road and the bouncing motodoub. But that didn't matter in the least to me, because the moment had been unforgettable. I had successfully run my first long-distance race.

Seav Houng was one of my brightest nieces, serious and a hard worker. This was the first time that we had the opportunity to become close. I discovered how much she looked up to me, and how she was quietly inspired by my achievements over the years. Chhay, half-displeased with this relationship, used to joke that I'd contaminated his daughter and made her obstinate and determined. Later, in 2009, Seav Houng got a scholarship to the American college Mount Holyoke, then one to Harvard Graduate School of Arts and Sciences. In April 2018, she defended her PhD thesis and began work on an MD in Singapore. I only wish I could have "contaminated" more of my family members!

-10-
New York: Mount Sinai and My First Marathon

By the end of 2006, I had received two offers for post-doctoral fellowships: one in Sydney and one in New York, at Mount Sinai School of Medicine. The Sydney project would continue my PhD research on HIV and drug resistance. The team there was also working with Cambodian patients. However, I was advised that it would be better to take the Mount Sinai offer, to avoid academic conflicts of interest with the IPC.

When I told my sister Heang that I was going to New York, she was surprised and a little shocked. Now that I had my PhD in hand, she had expected me to start working, make a good living, and at last start my own family, especially since Pierre and I had built a big house for that very purpose. Now she told me: "When you're finished with your studies, you'll be at the age of retirement!" Indeed, I was going on 35 years old now. For Cambodians, it was nearly too old to have children.

But I set off for New York, arriving in March 2007. I took my place among an army of postdoc researchers at Mount Sinai lab.

Right I faced a sort of academic culture shock. In New York, the research subjects were more fundamental and theoretical than my previous studies in Cambodia, where I conducted applied research and field work close to patients. New York was also very competitive. Everything seemed to go at a fast pace, with an expectation of autonomy. Postdoc candidates usually had to work weekends to be productive enough to get grants. It was common to see them in a zombie state from sleep deprivation. Even at lunchtime, people wouldn't stop working. Many seemed to have only superficial friendships and relationships.

Everything was very expensive too. We had to pay for the amount of space we used in the lab, so we measured closely and made every costly inch count. The "principal investigators" who ran projects had to continuously submit research proposals, update them with newly generated data, and then apply for more grants just to get money to keep the lab running. Half way through my stay, the global financial crisis hit, causing the U.S. government to cut back on non-military research budgets. As a result, some labs at Mount Sinai shut down entirely.

I realized very quickly that working in New York for the rest of my life would not be healthy for me. Still, there were things I quite liked about this community: the freedom of thought, the way we shared facilities and even the basic chemicals of our work. If you had any doubts, or just needed a hug, people were mostly happy to help. And if an expert couldn't be found at Mount Sinai, we would find one at another university in the United States.

Periodically we presented our research progress to the group, followed by a discussion. Special guests frequently came to give talks at free lunches, and we all could ask questions. I was amazed to see so many passionate researchers and new, eccentric subjects and inventions! It seemed anything was possible as long as you could round up the resources to translate your ground-breaking idea into an experimental project, and show that it was scientifically possible.

Chris, my mentor, was a rare white American among the principal investigators, or PIs, as we called them. He came from Harvard University. We worked in a very small space, struggling to make ends meet. Chris applied his engineering skills to the money problems. He often picked up materials that other labs were throwing away, such as laboratory shakers, rocker machines, a bench centrifuge and chairs. He fixed them up so that we wouldn't need to buy new ones. He actually set up a manual plate washer so well that the next lab over preferred to use ours rather than their automatic one.

I kept up with my running in New York. Running was a good way to keep physically fit, of course, but I was also learning its powers to dissipate stress, provide catharsis, and keep mind and body in healthy balance. There were times I really needed these curative effects, for example, when we got bad results from experiments that had taken days to set up. And I quickly found that, to my surprise, New York was a city of runners, home of the famous New York City Marathon.

I was very lucky to get student housing at Mount Sinai and live right in Manhattan. My place was on the 4th floor of a rather old apartment building on 97th street, between Park and Madison Avenues. I was only one and a half blocks from Central Park (one of my main running locales) and a block from the laboratory, which saved me time and money. My apartment was very small, and the building too old to have a lift, but in one of the world's most costly cities, I knew very well how fortunate I was.

For the first two weeks, Chris gave me afternoons off to go out and buy furniture and set up my new living space. Most incoming postdocs bought their furniture from outgoing ones at moving sales. Prices were nice and low. However, not all furniture was available this way. I had no bed, so Chris lent me an inflatable bed he used for his guests. Every time I moved in the night, it made a noise like rubbing on a plastic buoy. After sleeping this way for a couple of weeks, I knew I had to change: Pierre was coming to visit me. So I went to a clearance furniture shop and bought a fancy queen size, memory foam mattress and a bed frame with drawers underneath, for extra storage space. At Ikea I bought a set of folding table and chairs. I was especially happy because the price was good and delivery was free.

When the bed arrived, I came downstairs to meet the delivery men. They unloaded everything and left it on the sidewalk by the door. I gently asked if they could help carry it up to my apartment. They asked if there was a lift and which floor? When I said "no lift" and "fourth floor," they announced I'd have to pay extra—$10 per floor.

My jaw dropped. What a welcome to Manhattan, the "City that Never Sleeps."

I told the delivery men no, so they left the furniture out on the street. I called some of my postdoc friends to come lend some muscle.

This was the first time that New York's customs had blindsided me. When I first arrived, I had never had to tip anyone before. So, when taxi drivers told me the price of the ride, I gave them exactly what they asked for. It wasn't until I'd been there for a while that one driver finally looked at me after I'd paid and asked, "Where's my tip?"

I was horrified! I hadn't realized that tipping was mandatory here. Had all those other taxi drivers just stayed silent because they didn't want to make a scene, but secretly thought I was rude or cheap? But I soon learned the etiquette of American tipping, in taxis and restaurants and other places.

#

As for my studies, lots of people were working at that time on researching H1N1, or bird flu, because there had been a recent outbreak and it was frequently in the news. Chris and I were going to join in that effort, but we had to try and set ourselves apart. Chris had already done specialist work in immune system evolution. He knew about the mammal antigen CD1, which is very potent in boosting the immune response. But he—and everyone else—knew very little about bird CD1 and CD2. Now Chris had an original and challenging project in mind— he wanted to explore our ancestor the chicken's CD1 and CD2 genetics. This could be useful in the future for a bird flu vaccine, to improve birds' immune response to avian influenza, including the highly pathogenic H5N1, and so cut down the risk of transmission to humans.

The problem was that this required chickens. The lab and our budget were far too small for a chicken coop.

So we improvised. Chicken spleen cells were very important in this work, so before each experiment, I went to a live poultry market in Harlem. I walked all the way to save money on transportation, carrying the lab's icebox and a transport medium for the spleen.

At the poultry market, I had the vendors kill chickens for me. Depending on the day and the experiment, I might ask them to kill one bird, or several. I followed them into the slaughter room to show them where the spleen was, and to make sure that they properly extracted the organ to avoid contamination. Then I put the tissue safely in a tube with the transport medium. The rest of the chicken's body went into a set of processing machines, emerging featherless, and emptied of its organs, and clean.

From there, I rushed back to the lab to process the spleen and extract the leucocytes, a type of colorless cell, that we needed for our experiments. If I took too long, we wouldn't be able to use the cells, and I'd have to go all the way back.

So, the spleen went to the cause of science, the rest of the bird to the cause of fine dining. Often I cooked up a chicken dish for Chris or other friends.

#

There was one thing I especially liked about living in New York City: Because it had so many people from so many countries and cultures, I never felt discriminated against. There were people from Puerto Rico, Mexico, India, and the Middle East. And Cambodia. But when meeting people for the first time and telling them where I was from, I usually sensed they knew next to nothing about my country. Some said they had heard of it, but only through the tragic events of the Khmer Rouge. Some were better informed, but that usually meant they knew specifics about negative things—human rights violations, war crimes trials, human trafficking, poverty, corrupt government. Very few had been to Cambodia and experienced places like Angkor Wat. I always felt privileged to be the first Cambodian that they met. I made it my responsibility to tell them that travel to Cambodia was safe, and about the places they should visit. I also told them about the kindness and generosity of Cambodians, especially people in the countryside.

People came to New York because it was the city of opportunity. As the song says—"If I can make it there, I'll make it anywhere." That became one of my mantras. Unlike in France, nobody cared if you spoke with an accent or made grammatical errors. Nobody cared if you didn't look like them. You could hear many different languages just by walking down the street. You could eat food from all over the world. Being a foreigner was not an issue here, as long as you could contribute. Acceptance came from ability, innovation and hard work, not your ethnic group.

But it did lead to some interesting culture quirks in the labs. We had PIs from different parts of the world—China, Hong Kong, France, and Brazil, as well as Chris from the USA. And each PI tended to hire postdocs only from his or her own country. It felt like we had the whole world on our one floor, separated into little countries just like the real world was.

I lived across the street from an Indian postdoc named Nishay, who worked in the same floor as me, but under a different and very senior PI, the co-director of the Immunity Center. This PI had a reputation for being very harsh. His postdocs were often overworked and miserable. We often joked about how his lab was an empire, and how many grants he was bringing in to afford so much lab space. All his postdocs worked long hours for low pay, but he paid them the very least that he was allowed, and threatened to fire them if they didn't keep up. Many people in his lab left as soon as they had the chance.

It was particularly tough for Nishay, who had just moved to America with his wife and their new child. Three of them were living in an apartment the same size as mine—barely big enough for one person! His wife was out of work while she looked after their child, but after she did get a job, her entire pay check went towards day care for the boy. Add to that the fact that postdocs could be fired without notice or severance pay. So Nishay worked late nights and weekends, just to keep up with what his PI expected of him.

So I often shared the spleenless chicken I cooked with Nishay and his family. In return, Nishay passed along some of his best Indian music and Bollywood songs, which I would listen to on my long runs.

Eventually, Nishay brought his mother-in-law over to look after the child, so they wouldn't have to spend money on day care. But now there were four people in that small space. That was life in New York City—it was tough to survive.

In contrast, I was very lucky to have Chris as my PI. He was under the same pressure as anyone to get results, but he didn't try to unload it all onto me like some other PIs did. We both felt pressure, and it was easier to bear knowing that we were working together with the same load.

It was very different from how things worked in France, where the government provided a living allowance and researchers didn't have to constantly fight for grants in order to live.

#

While I did my postdoc, Pierre finished his appointment with the World Bank and went back to MIT to complete his PhD. Finally, we were back on the same continent—and MIT was only four hours away by bus.

However, something was going wrong, and I began to be concerned. When we were together, it seemed he was never really happy or emotionally connected. He did not enthusiastically support me like he once had. He tuned me out when I talked to him about my postdoc or running. To him, I found out, my running was useless, like a goldfish swimming circles in an aquarium. I asked him several times what was wrong, but he wouldn't engage. I was searching for his support, affection and love to help me cope with the challenges of living in New York. Once he just told me, "What are you complaining about? Many people have it much worse!"

He was right, of course, but it wasn't the answer I was expecting.

Then I found out what was wrong. He'd been getting up early to chat with someone on his laptop while I was asleep. This seemed odd. After a while, I did what many people would do: I read the chats. I confronted him. He confessed. He had met another woman while he was working in Zambia with the World Bank. He had been planning to ask her to marry him, and if she said yes, to end our marriage.

I was devastated. It was really the dishonesty that hurt me the most. If he had fallen in love with someone else and told me—or just fallen out of love with me—that would have been one thing. But knowing that I, his wife, had become his second choice of partner, that he had somehow seen himself remaining with me if the other women said no, was something I couldn't stand.

I told him I would be his second choice no longer. I wanted a divorce.

He went back to MIT. I went through a long period of crying. My thoughts grew dark. I reached out to him, though it was emotionally painful, trying to understand why this had happened. We had travelled the world; we had built up our confidence together. We felt proud of our achievements. Yet now I was depressed and sad and had lost my confidence.

I felt foolish and naïve. When I was on my own in Cambodia, other men, even married ones, often tried to flirt with me. They would ask me, "What, don't you think your husband is having an affair, flirting with other women while he's away?" I always said no, I'm certain he isn't. I thought they were being unfair to men, assuming they would all be unfaithful if given the chance.

My moral values and Catholic upbringing made me feel guilty and ashamed about getting a divorce. It meant rank failure, I thought. I had to repeat the word over and over again to myself so that it stopped sounding wrong. I found a little comfort in seeing the statistic that in the United States about half of all couples get divorced.

The morning after I told Pierre I wanted a divorce, I showed up late at the lab, with a miserable face and swollen eyes. It was all very embarrassing, because the lab spaces were open, and we could all see each other. Every time my colleagues saw me looking this way, I felt sorry for myself and started an avalanche of crying. I didn't try to explain—everyone was very busy and didn't need something else to worry about. Sometimes I retreated to the only space I could hide in, the tiny tissue culture room. I put music on my iPod. I cried, or felt angry, or dreamed of a better place, depending on which song was playing.

There weren't many people I could confide in. Sometimes I called maman, though. We had stayed in touch. All four of her other children had already divorced, so she had a different perspective. She tried to help me calm down, and told me that she was sorry it had happened. I think she was relieved that Pierre and I remained respectful of each other, and hadn't had children, so the divorce wasn't messy like my French siblings' divorces had been.

At 35, I was one of the oldest people in the lab. I was at a very different stage of life than the young ones, though I was good friends with them anyway. Many were still dating, or going to bars for one-night stands, not even thinking about marriage. With time I began to remember some of the advantages of being single. Now I could travel anywhere I wanted, whenever I wanted, without having to worry about another person's preferences or plans. I made new friends at my running club and sometimes they asked me to join them for a weekend outside the city or visit their countryside houses. Meanwhile, my lab research was yielding good results for publication. My running was improving. Slowly, slowly, my confidence began to grow.

On Netflix, I ordered the TV series "Sex and the City." I decided I would start to date again. I would put myself first for a while.

#

I have always been an extremely sensitive person, tender and even needy. Yet People often see me as peppy, and strong-minded or tough. In public, I try to share only the best parts of my emotions, and not reveal much of my weaker side. But with some things I just can't control my emotions. When I'm watching movies, I easily identify with the characters, and cry easily over them. It doesn't matter if it's a comedy, a romance, or even a Disney cartoon. I will usually end up with tears, using up entire boxes of tissues. I prefer to watch movies alone at home, because when I have a movie date or watch on an airplane, it's very embarrassing to get so worked up. People must think I got some bad news, seeing how much I cry!

One weekend in New York, I ordered some more movies through Netflix. "Run, Fat Boy, Run" triggered a mixture of tears and laughter, but "Rocky," "Nights in Rodanthe," "Enchanted" and "An Affair to Remember" affected me so strongly that after I watched each of them, I could barely recognize myself in the mirror. My face was so swollen, my eyelids so puffy, that I looked like a boxer after a big fight. I had to put ice on my eyelids, and wait a while before I dared to show myself at the lab.

I don't remember how old I was when I started to be so deeply affected by things, but it has only seemed to increase as I've gotten older. These moods are more painful, more frequent, and less predictable. I can get so preoccupied with suffering that I can't sleep. Even if I hear a story from a complete stranger on my travels, I can cry my eyes out. I cry at positive things, too. I connect easily with strangers, especially if they show me affection. The simplest things can move me to tears: Unexpected gifts or kindnesses, or people going out of their way to help me. Of course, I always cry more when I am busy, or stressed, as I was pretty often in New York City. The place was noisy and crowded, but at the same time, I often felt so lonely. Then, the divorce happened and I was suddenly even lonelier, desperately looking for meaning in my life, feeling worthless and naïve. I had to reorganize my whole life.

#

After the divorce, I was sometimes visited by some of my and Pierre's mutual friends, one I'd gotten to know when Pierre was living in Vancouver. They told me they wanted to come and check on me.

My apartment was tiny, and it was hard to fit them in—they were all very large men. They were very nice to me, and I was glad to see them again, but some things seemed a little odd.

One of them did sit-ups in the morning, sitting below my bed with his shirt off, wearing only underwear, showing off his slack abs. Another started asking me questions about dating: "How do I find a girlfriend and make her interested in me?"

After a while I concluded they were maybe trying to gauge my interest now that I was single. I was glad they didn't come out and directly ask me—I wasn't attracted to any of them, partially because starting a relationship with one of Pierre's friends would remind me too much of Pierre. But it was funny how these men would gingerly test the water just in case I might be wanting another relationship.

#

Emilie was one of my better friends among the other postdocs. She was a young, liberated woman, who liked to go out clubbing. I hadn't even heard of a "one-night stand" or "friends with benefits" before I arrived. Emilie told me stories about getting so drunk that when she woke up the next morning with a man she couldn't remember what his face looked like. I couldn't imagine doing something like that.

But she was determined to help me "have a good time," so one night I went partying with her. I tried to enjoy it, but I couldn't stand the deafening music and noise. You had to shout to talk to each other, and the heavy smoke suffocated me! On top of that, I was not an alcohol drinker. I just wanted to get out of the club as fast as possible. So I left Emilie there and went home.

When she invited me out again, I told her no thanks.

Some friends suggested I should sign up for online dating, but I never did that. I was perhaps too traditional—I preferred to encounter someone in the old-fashioned natural way. I liked the sudden rise of magical feelings and physical attraction.

From time to time, I still felt betrayed that Pierre had left, and I still felt foolish. I wanted to accelerate the process of healing by dating. I decided from then on, it would be better to be the "other woman" than the unwitting wife of a cheater.

At around this time, I took a membership at one of the biggest gyms near Mount Sinai, the 92Y. They had volleyball games once a week and I sometimes took part. I noticed a nice and quite handsome guy on the opposing team, who always seemed to serve strongly to me. It seemed he loved to see me running after the ball to return his serve. When I had trouble, he laughed, then served again even harder to challenge me! With time, there was a rapport between us. He always managed to be on the opposing team, serving to me. I started to like the challenge, and felt attracted by his sly, conniving smile.

One day, we crossed paths on the street outside my apartment. Having him in front of me, I could only feel awkward. I didn't know whether I wanted to hug and kiss him at once, or take to my heels and disappear into my building. He asked if I wanted to have a drink with him, but because I was so excited and confused at seeing him unexpectedly, I automatically responded that I didn't drink alcohol, only tea. He went on his way without suggesting an alternative.

Idiot, idiot! All the way up to my apartment, I was scolding myself that way. I realized I had misunderstood the language of dating in New York and missed my opportunity. I had turned him down without meaning to. It was my fault, though my inner voice told me if he'd been really interested he would have insisted.

I decided I would talk to him the next time we met on the volleyball court, and suggest getting together, but when the time came I was too scared. Later, I ran into him at Mount Sinai's gynecology department. It was a great surprise to learn that he was also at the school. My heart beat so fast, and I felt so confused that I could barely meet his eyes when we were talking. I knew I was acting very weird and uncomfortable. Maybe I was scared of falling in love.

Soon after, he sent me a friendly e-mail telling me that he was going to leave Mount Sinai for a job on the West Coast. I sat in my apartment reading it over and crying. I wished I could go back in time and grab my opportunity.

But without being aware of it, he had helped me through a very difficult time. When I'd been feeling depressed, I had managed to drag myself to the gym only because of the chance to see him there.

After a while, I started to date Jim, whom I'd met through running. He was much older than me, good looking, with high spirits, and at first all was wonderful. But not long into the relationship, I found some pictures and a hotel bill from a weekend he had spent away with another woman! On top of that, he had lied to me about it. That weekend he left me in a hurry, saying he had to visit his mother, who was in the hospital gravely ill.

I felt that I'd been a fool. I rejected all of his apologies and told him I wanted no more contact with him. But Jim was unbelievably persistent in trying to regain my affection. Still, I didn't reply to his calls, messages or e-mails. I even managed to avoid seeing him at our running club by changing my schedule.

One day, Jim surprised all my colleagues by showing up on the 7th floor at my lab bench. His face had a half sorry and half hopeful expression. He handed me a folded t-shirt, saying, "You forgot this!" with a smile. It was the large cotton t-shirt I used to sleep in. Then he gave me a big, elegant bouquet of red roses, mixed with baby's breath, and a little note saying "I'm so sorry!"

I grabbed my t-shirt, left the flowers in his hands, and told him to leave immediately. He withdrew, as I tried to hide silent tears from my colleagues.

But a bit later, one of the senior female scientists came in and informed me there was a gentleman with flowers waiting for me in the corridor. My face began to flush. It felt like a panic attack was coming on. Jim hadn't left the building after all! He was just outside, unashamed, exposed to everyone in sight, waiting for me.

Some of my colleagues found it all amusing. They asked me what was going on. Some must have thought I was cold-hearted, insensitive to such an impassioned declaration of love. News of the incident spread quickly. For the next few days, my colleagues would joke about it whenever they met me in the elevator, and my friends from other floors teased me about the gentleman who came with roses to declare his love at the lab bench.

Eventually I relented. I was living like a real New Yorker now. I took Jim back, though now it was more like "friends with benefits" than a long-term commitment. I also started dating a new, good-looking man, who lived most of the time in Long Island, where he surfed. I met him at the annual fundraising dinner for the Angkor Hospital for Children in Cambodia. I had been helping them gather donations in the New York area, which allowed me to meet other Cambodian-Americans in New York. As it happened, my friend Emilie was also at that dinner. She agreed that this surfer man was charming. He reminded her of Hugh Grant. Once in a while, Emilie would ask how things were going with "Hugh Grant," and I had to tell her the truth—his performance did not live up to expectations! Besides, dating two guys at the same time was too confusing for me. I said I would keep on with Jim, and gave her the green light to try her luck with "Hugh Grant." In the end, we had some good laughs, talking about our issues with men. I avoided any relationship that could become serious and compromise my commitment to return to Cambodia.

In ways like this, I tried to enjoy the freedom of being single. But in some ways it was difficult—I had been betrayed by men twice now, and I was a sensitive person to begin with. I still don't know if I harbored PTSD from my childhood under the Khmer Rouge, or if I'd been scarred long-term by being orphaned in France and living with a foster family, but I was very insecure with Jim. Whenever we said goodbye at the subway station, where Jim took the train back to his apartment and I went back to mine, I wondered if he was going off to see another woman again. He swore he had broken it off with that other girl, but I just couldn't fully trust him anymore.

When Jim wanted to, he could be very charming, romantic and sweet. My inner voice continued to warn me: "Don't be foolish—this is a game to trap you!" So I remained cool. Jim would take me to see ballets, operas and Broadway shows. He knew I liked eating even more after a hard training session, so he often cooked healthy, tasty meals for me, or delicious cranberry scones that I could bring to the lab when I was too busy to cook good meals for myself. Jim was divorced—his former wife had been Australian, CEO of a sizeable company. He'd gotten enough money from the divorce settlement that he didn't really need to work, so he had plenty of free time to enjoy himself and spend with me.

After three years in New York, I reached the end of my postdoc. As I was getting ready to leave, Jim asked me to marry him. I could sell my house in Cambodia, he said, and stay in New York.

I told him, "I'm not interested right now."

#

I've mentioned that I ran in New York, but maybe haven't made clear how important it was to me. Especially after the divorce, running was like medicine and meditation. I dumped all my bad moods into running—all my frustration, my anger, my uncertainty, and my depression. I ran as formal training but at other times with no particular purpose at all. When I was in bad mood, I ran fast, not worrying about how many laps I had done.

Sometimes I felt my heart was going to explode—it was beating that fast and my breath was so short. Then, each time I survived a training run or race, I was surprised and proud to have overcome another tough challenge. The feeling of pushing myself hard and seeing myself constantly improve was satisfying to the extreme.

Central Park has lots of running paths, including the famous one around the big reservoir. One reservoir loop was about a mile and half. By the end of my postdoc, I had run so many miles in that park that it will always hold a special place in my heart.

In my second year in New York, I joined the New York Flyers running club. When we ran races, we wore our club t-shirts so that the club photographers could spot us, take pictures and upload photos onto the club website. Every race, the top five men and women in the club were lauded on the website. At first, I had no idea that this page existed. I was just showing up, running and going home or to the lab. Other runners often headed to dinner or happy hour drinks together, but not me.

Then, the club asked for volunteers to be pacers at a New York City marathon training session. A pacer is someone who picks a comfortable pace and runs in front of a group of runners to make sure they keep a consistent speed the entire distance. Sometimes the pacer gives them encouraging words.

When I went to collect my pacer t-shirt, with the words "Follow me" on back, the club president declared: "It's you! Nary Ly! Speedy Gonzales!"

I was stunned. It was a huge club. How did she know me? I'd been in the top five female runners several times, and had been listed on the website, but there was never a photograph of me. In effect I had been running incognito, so the president was excited to finally put a face on my name.

I felt so happy to be part of the club—and respected for my running ability.

In 2008, the Olympics were held in Beijing. I hadn't really paid much attention to the games before, but in New York City, everyone was very into them. People were constantly updating each other on Team USA's performance, the latest news and videos, and predictions for coming events. I started to be curious, especially about the long-distance events. I read and watched videos. I learned of a male marathon runner from Cambodia. His name was Bunting Hem. He was the first person from Cambodia ever to compete in that event.

After I had been running for a while, I told a coach at the New York Flyers that I'd given myself a new goal. I wanted to run my first marathon. If I could make it to the finish line, I told the coach, my next goal would be to represent Cambodia at the Olympic games, as there had never yet been a female Olympian marathoner from my country.

Maybe it was my incoherent explanation, or maybe it was a wacky goal, but the coach gently said, "Yes, it's a nice dream." I was disappointed. I felt like he was patting me on the head and calling me a good little girl. I felt so deflated that I decided to keep the dream to myself from now on.

Before running a full marathon, I would need to improve my performance in a half. My 1 hour 54 minute result in the Siem Reap race had been slow, so I joined a speed training class. One day, after a training session, the coach told me to get a stopwatch to time myself. At that point, I didn't have one, because with timers going beep-beep all day in the lab, I wanted to get away from them when I was running. So I acquired my first sophisticated stopwatch, a Garmin.

I kept training and ran the NYC half marathon in 2009 in 1 hour, 35 minutes, a big improvement. At the end of the year, the New York Flyers organized a gala. That year, I was very surprised to be named one of the "Young Rookies" of the year and receive a medal! Moments like this really helped my self-confidence and recovery from my divorce.

Occasionally, I volunteered on weekends to be the running partner of a blind man. Sharing my free time by guiding him and helping him experience the joy of running gave me a sense of warmth and purpose. I was giving back to this guy. I had had people supporting me at times of trial in my life; now I naturally connected with a man who needed my help. In addition to the emotional attachment, there was a physical one, a rope tether. We talked as we ran; I shared with him some thoughts on key areas of Central Park and the beautiful scenery.

At the very end of my postdoc, I confided my Olympic dream to one of my best female runner friends, and she showed great enthusiasm! I signed up for my first full marathon. I wanted to see if I was really capable of running 42 kilometers. I had run that half marathon in Siem Reap to celebrate the end of my PhD, and now I would run a full marathon to close out my postdoc. Scaling up like this seemed nicely symbolic. And of course there was the question of whether I could get any closer to my goal of being the first female Cambodian marathoner in the Olympic Games.

All my life, I have made and kept friends easily. For example, at La Haute Bercelle, I had to meet every six months with my "judge" Isabel, to show her my grades and prove I was doing well at school. Ten years after she retired from that position, she found my email address, and we got back in touch. I took some satisfaction in offering her a copy of my PhD after my thesis defense. We missed each other when she visited Cambodia but she came to meet me in New York during my postdoc. Even though she had once been in a position of authority over me, now we could speak easily as friends.

During my postdoc, I also got a visit from Prof. Durosoir. We spent a few hours catching up. He had come to New York for an event honoring his late father Lucien Durosoir, a remarkable composer and musician whose long career included service in the French army during World

War I, when he performed for his fellow soldiers in the trenches. His son, my professor, later published a book of his letters and compositions and helped create a scholarship at Yale University. Now there was going to be a concert—a Yale duet would play a program of French music including pieces by his father.

I never got the chance to tell Prof. Durosoir this, but I always considered him as a grandfather, and I sometimes wished he was my real grandfather. He was a very poetic man, and once in a while he would get in touch and make sure I was doing well. He always gave me good and sincere advice, as he would do for his own daughters.

I told him all about the divorce, my personal views about living in New York City and dating. I told him I felt I was too naïve and vulnerable for the city, and that I was overwhelmed. When I finished, he told me that I was a special and rare person nowadays: a person who was moral and tried to do the right thing. But, he explained that, at the same time, I hurt myself by being moral. He said it was beautiful, in a way, but it would also be painful for me.

I didn't understand at the time, but I do now.

I also had a visit from my PhD mentor, Prof. Fleury of Bordeaux-2, who arrived with his family. They took me to a dinner with jazz music, and we had a wonderful time catching up.

I'm very fortunate and grateful that these people kept in contact with me over the years. Often, because I moved so much and because I had lost contact with my real families, both Cambodian and French, I felt like I didn't have a family at all. These people whom I met, and the people whom I worked with, became like an extended family to me.

For this reason, I always felt it deeply when my postdoc friends left to go back to their own countries. It seemed like a separation, or like they were abandoning me. My inner voice would tell me that I'd never see them again. I often cried at these departures.

#

While I worked on my postdoc, I had been in contact with the head of the IPC virology unit back in Cambodia, to which I was slated to return. He had kept my position for me during my leave of absence.

I wanted to return to help improve the corps of local Cambodian scientists. I was also discussing potential research projects with IPC, and the possibility of collaborating on them with the Mount Sinai teams. At the time, the World Health Organization was on alert about HPAI, a type of bird flu, and the public was panicking. As a result, there was a lot of funding for HPAI research. HPAI originated in East Asia, and since I'd be in Cambodia, I would be close to patients and animals under study.

However, the head of IPC told me I couldn't wait till the end of my postdoc to come back. The Australian postdoc at IPC had had a family emergency and had to leave, so they needed me to come right away and take over the project. I suggested an alternative: that I would visit Cambodia for a few days for the position handover and then return to New York to finish my postdoc project. After submitting my manuscript, I could return to Phnom Penh and officially resume working at IPC.

Since the short-term trip would be expressly for the benefit of IPC, I asked that it pay for my airplane tickets and other expenses. To my astonishment, the virology manager refused. He said I had to work it out with Mount Sinai. I was surprised too that the director of IPC, who was copied in on all the e-mails, didn't intervene. I felt completely dismissed.

I was offended again when we talked about the position I would have. I had now studied at prestigious universities in France and the United States, obtained a PhD with the highest honor and collaborated with eminent U.S. labs in postdoc research. I expected this would mean a better position and a better salary. But no: I was told that I would only get my old salary.

It was humiliating. The colonial mentality, it seemed, was still alive and well at Institut Pasteur. The values of the founder Louis Pasteur were gone. The idea of local scientists becoming equal to their French research colleagues was just Prof. Durosoir's dream. I had given nine years of hard work and dedication to IPC, yet I was still not considered an equal to French scientists.

I felt I had been naïve during all those years of loyal service and dedication. I had originally been lured to IPC with the promise of becoming a prominent Cambodian scientist who could do her own research. I had hoped that that might lead, down the road, to my having my own laboratory and research team, making a significant scientific discovery and perhaps even receiving a Nobel Prize. I could see now that none of this was going to happen. Talking further with IPC was pointless, fruitless. So I made up my mind: I would not go back to IPC.

However, I have always been an optimist at heart. I chose to recalibrate. I decided to focus on something I could do, rather than something I could not. I would become an independent woman, in charge of my own destiny. I would not be used or exploited. I would do my best to lead a serene and spiritual life in which I was in communion with nature.

#

With the marathon coming up, I treated myself to a wonderful cruise around the Hawaiian islands. It was part of the resolution I had made since my divorce—I was going to live my life for me.

The *Pride of America* took us to four islands in seven days. The ship had four levels—it was utterly gigantic. Usually cabins were shared by two people but I paid extra to have one all to myself. I didn't want to share a sleeping space with someone I didn't know.

Every morning, I got up at five to do my running training on a treadmill; usually I was the only one in the ship's gym at this time. I'm sure most people thought I was a little strange. A woman on her own, without a husband or boyfriend, spending her time on the cruise running and exercising, rather than relaxing?

The ship would stop at a destination during the day, and move on at night. Each morning we woke up in a new place. I paid for extra activities on land at each destination, and enjoyed lots of shipboard activities in the evening and early morning. There were always plenty of people to meet: locals, guides, other passengers. Every day I went out with a new group of people. I still keep in touch with some of the friends I made on that trip. I met two retired Australian women, Dianne and Janet, who had been friends since high school and who have since visited me in Cambodia.

#

But soon the cruise was over, and it came time to run my first marathon. I wanted to get a feeling of what my time could be. But mostly I just wanted to reach the finish line. I would use my performance to set a time goal for my next marathons, but for this first one, I would enjoy myself and have a chance to say goodbye to my friends, who would be waiting along the course to cheer me on. I would blow them kisses when I couldn't reach them. Jim would run with me for the last six miles, when I would need an extra boost and mental energy to cross the finish line. This was Jim's idea, as a nice end to our relationship. By now we both knew it would cease when I returned to Cambodia. This was the gentlemanly and sensitive side of him that I had always appreciated. However, Jim would have to leave me a few yards before the finish line, because he wasn't enrolled in the race and security wouldn't let him near the finish line.

Once again, I thought of my palm reading and the prediction that I would die young. What if I died in the marathon? However, I felt I would be happy knowing that, at 37, I had died testing my body's ability and trying to achieve something new.

Early on the day of the race, I met up with some New York Flyers friends, and we took the ferry together to Staten Island, where the race starts. Some of them had previously run it; they guided me through the bus shuttle and warm-up. We got out of our street clothes. We put on big plastic bags over our running clothes to keep us warm, because it's cold in New York in November. We cut a bit out of the bottom of the bag for our head, and two holes on the side for our arms. My bag was an unusual one, a strong, transparent pink one from the lab. Under it I was wearing a long-sleeve shirt, and old socks as gloves. We would start the race bundled up, and abandon these layers en route as we warmed up.

We took our places near the starting line. The freezing wind and weather kept us packed together like penguins for warmth. There was music and entertainment, speeches from the organizers, and finally a speech from Mayor Michael Bloomberg.

The gun went off, and we began to run.

I was lucky that my starting wave was just after the elites, so I didn't have to go through the first two miles of road dodging the fruit peels, plastic bags and clothes which the thousands of front runners ahead had discarded—to say nothing of running over their pee! (It's one of the marathon world's "dirty secrets" that serious runners, having waited for extended periods at the starting line, sometimes empty their bladders in the first few strides of a race.)

It was thrilling to see so many runners and groups from so many different countries. The huge crowd of spectators gave me extra joy. We crossed one by one the five boroughs of New York (Staten Island, Brooklyn, Queens, the Bronx and Manhattan). At various points we were greeted with intense cheering and bands pumping out some very loud music. At mile 18, NYF club members were waiting to cheer us on and hand out power gels. Then I saw Jim, who with his happy smile started to pace me, and I felt strong again.

At 92nd Street and First Avenue, just before entering Central Park, friends from Mount Sinai were waiting for me. Helene from France and her boyfriend Pablo were holding a big board with my name in capital letters to make sure that I would not miss it. *NARY vas-y!* (Go Nary!).

My niece, Seav Houng, who had given me that all-important boost in my first race in Siem Reap, was also there (she was studying at Mount Holyoke College in Massachusetts at the time), with my postdoc mentor Chris. But it wasn't just friends who knew my name. Before the race, Jim had suggested that I write it on my running T-shirt. This had the desired effect. Complete strangers chanted, "Nary, Nary!" as I passed.

As I ran, I had a powerful feeling of wellbeing and peace in myself. If I had died right there, I would have had no regrets. But melancholic thoughts were arising in my mind too. After all, I was ending the New York part of my life. Indeed, when I drew close to the finish line, with only two miles to go, I wished I could freeze time. I wished I could retain my elation forever.

As we passed through Central Park, the crowd was frenetic, yelling and giving us signs and blessings. I felt the warmest love even from strangers. Over the security barriers, I high-fived people I had never met before. By now I had forgotten about pacing myself—I just really wanted to reach the Tavern on the Green, the end of the 26-mile race!

I passed under the finish arch with a time of 3 hours, 34 minutes.

Jim was very happy with that time. But he said it would have been much lower if I'd run straight in the middle of the road, rather than zigzagging to hug friends, blow kisses and entertain the crowd. But I wouldn't have done it any differently.

No doubt, there was major room for improvement. Having looked at the times of various female Olympic marathoners, I knew that even if I could cut my time to three hours I would still be at the back of the group. But I took some comfort in knowing that 15-20 percent of participants didn't finish at all.

#

It was time to depart New York now. As I packed, I felt a twinge of regret leaving Chris behind at the lab. The next year, he ran out of funds, and had to shut down the research. Fortunately, he found a good position at one of the pharmaceutical companies in New York City.

—Part Five—

A Khmer Rouge Survivor's Revenge

-11-
Cambodian National Athlete, Training at the Home of Champions

Now I had to plan my life as a single person. I went back to Cambodia to focus on a new goal that I had set for myself. I would reduce my marathon time to three hours. I would develop this gift that I had discovered in myself—my running ability—in order to become independent and self-sufficient. That seed of an idea began to take root and germinate.

Running was an activity to which I could commit myself fully. It depended on me alone. And yet it could have effects beyond me. If I could make my way to the Olympic arena, it would show that a small country could arise triumphantly from a dark period. We could be equal to the developed countries! It didn't matter how small we were—what was important was our accomplishments. The founder of the Olympic Games Committee, Pierre de Coubertin, once said, in a quote that has always resonated with me: "The most important thing in the Olympic games is not to win, but to take part, just as the most important thing in life is not the triumph but the struggle. The essential thing is not to have conquered but to have fought well."

I knew deep inside that I was making the right choice, but I had to be realistic. I was back in Cambodia without a job and income.

I had a small amount of savings from my postdoc, and I had rented my house out while I was in New York, so I had some money from that. But I would need more help. I would try to get myself designated as a "national athlete," an amateur recognized by the government as a potential contender in international competitions. A small stipend comes with this title.

To that end, I managed to obtain a meeting with the Cambodian Minister of Education and Sport. I explained that I wanted to become a national athlete. I recognized that my current ability would not get me a gold medal at the next Olympics. My goal was not to be on the podium, but to finish the race as the first Cambodian female Olympian marathoner and inspire the young generation, especially girls, and bring pride to our country. I would train for the next two years to bring my marathon time down to three hours.

The minister seemed convinced by my strategy. He sent word to the Khmer Amateur Athletics Federation (KAAF) to process my documents. Later I met the federation's secretary general and his staff. I became a national athlete. So far, so good.

Then, at the Olympic Stadium in Phnom Penh, I met Hem Bunting, the Beijing games Olympian whom I had heard of in New York. He had been a national athlete for quite some time by then. Bunting came from a poor farming family in Stung Treng province; he had nine siblings. He was totally devoted to running. He trained constantly, and slept at the Olympic Arena's National Sport Centre dormitory, a rather creepy place that was falling apart.

Right away, showing me around the stadium, he displayed his enthusiasm for finally having a female athlete with whom he could train. He also opened my eyes to the realities of being a national athlete in Cambodia. He told me all about the various bureaucratic difficulties he'd encountered.

At the time, the salary for a national athlete was $70 per month—not even enough to pay for gas between my house and the Olympic stadium, where I trained. Small as the salary was, it wasn't even reliable. According to Bunting, there were often problems getting it. He informed me when it was time to go and get my first payment and accompanied me to the sport centre office. He said I should always count the money (which was in Cambodian Riels–4,000 to the U.S. dollar—so there was quite a lot to count). Often our salaries were delayed for two weeks, if they didn't go missing entirely. However, everyone at the office knew Bunting, and they knew he could have a hot temper, so they didn't dare mess around with his pay. Having Bunting with me guaranteed I would get mine too.

But this support would only last six months. Clearly I would need to find some other way of getting money.

Sport in general wasn't a big part of Cambodian culture. It was generally viewed as for the young and people from the countryside. When I told my sister, Heang, that I was not going back to the IPC, that I would be a national athlete, I got a sermon from her. She was overwhelmed by my stupidity! "Why did you pursue all those long studies just to be a national athlete? You may love your nation, but your nation doesn't care about you!"

I understood her reaction, so I let her give the lecture. Then I explained what had happened to me at IPC, and all my reasons for wanting to become a national athlete. I thought that if I made her understand, and so would the rest of my family.

After that, I stopped trying to explain myself and just focused on trying to achieve my goal. I kept the Olympic part of the goal to myself, worried that making it public would compromise it. It would be my secret objective.

To help me out, sometimes other national athletes would give me lifts home on their motorbikes. Other times, I ran all the way, a distance of eight kilometers.

The long hours under the strong Cambodian sun tanned me—I got dark patches all over my face and a dark brown body. I became thinner, my breasts smaller. In Cambodia, this was at odds with local beauty standards, which valorized white skin and a buxom body. I'm sure a lot of people thought I was ruining my looks, but I didn't care.

I always tried to start running early, at 5:15 am. That meant I had to wake up at 4:45. I hired a motodoub driver to drive alongside me as I ran and carry extra clothes, electrolyte drinks, and water to wash the salt off my face to prevent further damage to my skin. His headlight illuminated the streets in front of me when the sun had not yet risen. The streets were poorly lit, and there were many hazards: big potholes in the roads, frequent construction sites, and mountains of garbage. One extra role of the motodoub: fending off stray dogs. Cambodia has a very high rate of death from rabies, even though it's a preventable disease through vaccine and antiserum, but these are too expensive for most people, and most dogs aren't vaccinated.

Traffic could be dangerous as well. Drivers often wouldn't look out for pedestrians, let alone runners, and wouldn't stop if they hit you. They were only worried about hitting luxury cars, because people who drove them were rich and influential.

It was hardly an ideal way to train. But I kept with it and got better. I ran in national competitions in Kep, Pursat, Siem Reap and other provinces. I beat younger female runners, and at the international half marathons (there was as yet no full marathon in Cambodia), I often finished on the podium. I started to appear in the local news.

#

I had a house of my own, so rent wasn't a problem. However, I would have to eat, train, travel to racing events, pay a housekeeper and the motodoub driver, and pay for electricity, water and taxes. I'd also acquired a second-hand car. My new life would require at least $500 a month. The national athlete stipend would hardly make a dent in that sum.

I started looking for sponsorships. But in the meantime, I had to think of ways to become more self-sufficient. So I set up a garden and bought some animals—three goats (one male and two female, so they could reproduce), a pair of rabbits, two turkeys, two small dogs, chickens, geese and hundreds of baby tilapia for the pond. It was like Noah's Ark at my house!

Unfortunately, I didn't know very much about taking care of animals, which led to some very interesting lessons.

I set up coops for the poultry, tied the goats to one of the palm trees so they could graze but not eat the trees and vegetables, and put the rabbits in a hutch.

Things started to go wrong from there. The goats tangled up their ropes until they began to choke and bleat. I felt bad for them, and was embarrassed as well. What if my neighbors thought I was mistreating them? I wished I could give them more space to run around, but I had to keep them away from my vegetable garden.

Eventually, I could not stand hearing their incessant cries anymore and I did let them free. I built a fence out of wood and tree trunks around the garden, expecting that would hold them back, but I had underestimated my goats. I came home one day to find the housekeeper red-faced and overwhelmed. The goats had gotten inside the house! She had chased them, but they had run onto the terrace. We both tried to chase them back into the enclosure, but instead, they followed each other, waving their tails at us, breaking tiles and excreting everywhere as they ran. They jumped from the terrace to the awning over the door, then onto my car and scratching the paint! It was a nightmare.

The Phnom Penh half marathon was one of the races that I won. I used the prize money to build the goats a small, sophisticated house, from which they couldn't escape.

But there were other problems. The rabbits would get out into the grass, and the dogs would chase them. If the housekeeper or I were around, we could shoo the dogs away. The rabbits were smart, and usually hid under the house's water tank, where the dogs couldn't get them. So I thought it would be all right, but one day while we were away from the house, the dogs caught a rabbit, and left its intestines all over the yard.

Another day when we were in the house, we heard a loud bang from outside. Bang! Bang! Bang! At first we couldn't figure out what it was, but then we saw it: the male turkey was attacking our water tank. The tank was bright and reflective, so the turkey saw his reflection and thought it was a rival bird! He was standing in front of the tank, bobbing his head and pecking at the tank. He must have been so confused—every time he pecked the tank, he looked under it to see where the other bird had gone, but of course, he saw nothing. He'd lift his head again and suddenly, the rival bird was back! We were afraid he might hurt himself, so we chased him away from the tank. But that didn't work—he kept coming back, no matter how many times we chased him away.

The female turkey escaped, too. Even though we'd clipped her wings, she managed to fly over the house fence and we couldn't get her back.

The chickens and geese stayed nicely where they were supposed to, but during the dry season, they caught influenza because I hadn't had them vaccinated. I replaced only the chickens. Since some of the original chickens hadn't caught the disease, I interbred them, hoping to end up with a cluster of chickens that were immune to influenza.

I was glad to have my housekeeper living with me. I gave her the budget for the week, and she did all the shopping and made all our meals. She wasn't married at that time and had no children, and she took time off only twice every year, for important holidays, to go and visit her family in Prey Veng province. If she needed to go to them for any other reason, I would give her time off. Later, I hosted a provincial boy from Siem Reap, so that he could study at the university in Phnom Penh. In return, he helped the housekeeper.

We ate meals together like a family. It made the house feel a lot less lonely than if I had been living there on my own.

#

After a few months in Phnom Penh, I was becoming fed up with the training environment. The heavy traffic, starting at seven every morning, was becoming too much for me. I couldn't use the stadium for running when it rained, and even after it dried, foot falls in the soil track made it uneven, and there was a risk of twisting my ankles. This did happen to me once, and I couldn't run for several weeks. Moreover, there was no qualified national coach.

I had to find a better training environment and train with faster athletes.

I contacted the former coach of the New York Flyers, asking for suggestions. He gave me one that for me was totally out of the blue: Kenya, specifically the High Altitude Training Center (HATC) in Iten.

My first reaction was, "What?"

I knew that Kenya was famous for producing champion marathoners. But I had never been anywhere in Africa—I only knew it, or thought I did, from stories and the news. Back as a schoolgirl in France, one of my favorite books had been "The Lion King." My images of Kenya were of wild animals, Maasai costumes and dances, and Mount Kilimanjaro. But gradually I got used to the idea of going, and laid plans to spend three months at the center, from August to October 2010, then run the New York City marathon in the first week of November, to see how, or if, my time would improve if I would run in a straight line.

There was, of course, the question of how to pay for this. In the end it was my sister Heang who solved the problem. She had been the person most strongly opposed to my running professionally. She had barely even heard of the Olympics. But to my great surprise she agreed to help pay for the trip. Her actions showed that she really did care about me and want me to be happy. She had only said harsh things, because she wanted to try to protect me from making a mistake. I felt loved, and I appreciated her great help!

While I was in Kenya, she was also the only one who called me every so often, to check that I had not been eaten by a lion.

\#

Iten, "The Home of Champions," had not previously seen the likes of me. I was the first Cambodian to stay there, alone, and I was female. On top of that, I was a scientist with a PhD. I didn't act as serious as some of the other national athletes. I socialized with everyone. And I was the slowest runner at the camp, who nonetheless wanted to represent her country at the Olympic Games. I don't deny that some of them thought I was rather peculiar. I didn't mind—I'd have thought the same if I were them. The HATC was run by Lornah Kiplagat, a former long-distance runner who had set multiple records in her time. Her husband, Peter, was her coach and manager. I had arrived with a training program that I'd drawn up for myself. I wanted something tough. I would have only one rest day per week instead of two. But when Peter saw my program, he looked at me and asked if I had come to HATC for a vacation. To him it was a joke! Then he gave me a training program harder than anything I'd seen in my life.

I would run a peak distance per week of 180 kilometers. That meant I would often have to run twice per day—once in the morning at six, before breakfast, and once in the afternoon. Peter would fine tune my training program as needed. After nine weeks of this regimen, I would have a goal: To run my second marathon in New York in 3 hours 20 minutes, a 14-minute improvement over my first at 3 hours 34 minutes.

He did give me the first two weeks to take it easy and adapt to the high altitude. But after that, the ordeal began.

My daily life went like this: I started with an early run in the misty cold. Back at the camp, I soaked my heavy legs in the cold pool. I had a quick shower and then breakfast. Usually the buffet had porridge, hard-boiled eggs, bread (home-baked) with butter, jam, and peanut butter. There was a rotation between French toast, crepes, flapjacks and a Kenyan type of fried bread, hot water for instant coffee, hot chocolate or tea Chai.

After, I went to the gym for a bit under two hours. Then coffee or a snack, rest, then lunch. A typical lunch buffet included soup, rolls (baked in-house), rice, noodles or pasta with sauces and stews (predominantly vegetarian), and salad. After that, I took an afternoon nap or rest, then went for my second run, then to the gym for stretching and strengthening of the upper body and for special classes to strengthen core muscles. Then it was to the sauna or to just relax before dinner. The menu varied night to night, but included lots of hearty dishes such as beef stew, barbecue, chapati, and mashed potatoes. Then it was free time after dinner, relaxing or watching TV at the lounge. At 10 pm, I fell into bed and slept.

Mornings at HATC were usually cold with a thick mist. It was often difficult to find the motivation to get out of bed. To make it easier, I joined some female running groups, or brought a Kenyan running pacer along. Sometimes we ran on trails, whose red dust turned into sticky mud when it rained. Rain made training harder, because mud stuck to your shoes and made your feet heavier. We also ran on the area's many running paths, rocky ones, up and down hills. Sometimes I ran alone on the trails and got lost, but it was always possible to find a friendly local person to give me directions back.

As I built up my training, my body shaped up but I was continually sore—even massages were painful. With every run, my performance got better, but lactic acid accumulated in my legs so I often ran with stiff muscles and heavy legs. At night, my legs cramped up, and I'd get only a few fragmented hours of sleep. I was completely exhausted, and impatient for my days off. But even during days off from running, I still had to go to the gym for stretching and light exercises on the machines. On those days, I did spend time enjoying the sauna, though.

My Kenyan pacer believed that if I trained in Iten for six months, I could get my time to 2 hours 45 minutes. He was a great pacer and a very nice person, but I preferred a more realistic and safer approach, shaving off five minutes or so at a time. I just didn't think myself capable of jumping straight from 3 hours 34 minutes to 2 hours 45, even if I trained in Iten for a whole year. If I tried, I might end up seriously injuring myself.

Despite my acclimatization, it was difficult to catch my breath at that altitude. My heart pounded fast and hard as I ran. There were times I thought I was going to have a heart attack and die. Sometimes, I wondered if coming here had been a bad decision, if I should even have become an athlete in the first place. But each evening I would realize I had survived another day of training. I learned to take my training day by day.

Peter recommended that during my rest time I stay in the camp lying on the bed to rest my legs. But sometimes I escaped to visit the homes of Kenyan friends whom I'd made. I brought them food, sweet drinks, milk, sugar and meat as gifts. Once in a while, we cooked together at their house on a Sunday (most Kenyans go to church on Sundays, and they never trained on the Sabbath). We ate together on the ground, using our fingers when there weren't enough forks or spoons to go around. These friends showed me the forests, the waterfalls, the best places to view the Rift Valley, and the zoo.

Some foreign runners avoided spending time with the Kenyans. This was more than an issue of socializing: it was common for Kenyans to ask us foreigners for money or things such as stop watches, shoes, mobile phones, and running outfits. Some asked if they could clean our shoes and clothes, in return for money to buy food for their families. People told me I was too soft-hearted, but I tried to give as much as I could because I remembered being underprivileged. For me, asking for help was shameful, so if people did, I felt they must really need help. One Kenyan runner was a single mother of two children. I often visited her, and brought her gifts of basic things like oil, butter, sugar and clothes. Generally I tried to avoid giving money, but it was hard not to, when everyone was coming to me with sad stories—they needed money to bury a loved one, to buy medicine for a sick child, or help someone in the hospital. It broke my heart, and I even had trouble sleeping, wracked with guilt at my relative prosperity. Every time I gave them money, I told them it was the last time, but they always came back with even sadder stories. I knew that some of them had to be lying, but I couldn't help but wonder: What if it were true?

Finally it came time to leave HATC for New York. The night before, I had a nightmare that I mixed up the date and was panicking, desperately trying to find a way to arrive on time to run my marathon. The next morning, I said goodbye to Peter and told him about the nightmare. He smiled at me, half-laughing, and told me it was normal to be nervous. He gave me a last few pieces of advice for when I arrived in New York: Go quickly to pick up your bib at the Javits Convention Center. Don't stroll around at the marathon expo but go home and rest. You'll be fine, he told me. You've trained well.

In New York, I again experienced the euphoria that comes with starting a marathon with a huge throng of runners. We raced through streets that were now familiar to me. Things went well for me until near the end. For the first time, I experienced the horrible sensation, common among long-distance runners, known as "hitting the wall." It was a rapid, unexpected exhaustion, caused by my body running out of sugar to burn. I felt suddenly like I was going in slow motion, my legs moving more slowly, feeling heavier. My pace declined, but my brain was still working, and I ordered myself to keep going and push harder, telling myself to just put one foot in front of the other. Don't walk, don't stop! There were only a few more kilometers to the finish line. I had the sensation that I was running in clouds. My vision was blurring, and the crowds' cheers somehow seemed blurred, too. I didn't even have the energy to reach the power gel on my back. I was half numb. There were no cramps or physical pain, but keeping going was a terrible struggle, like trying to run in a swimming pool.

Finally I crossed the finish line. Despite "the wall," my time was 3 hours 16 minutes! Not only was this 18 minutes faster than my previous marathon, it was better than the 3 hours 20 minutes I was aiming for.

In every marathon, you learn a lesson. In this one, it was that I needed to properly fuel my body with glycogen sugar chains. In later races, I was always careful to take sports gels and white sugar cubes every five kilometers in the second half of the course.

#

Before heading back in Cambodia, I bought an advanced marathon training book. Once I got home, I followed the book's advice and made my own training program with pace calculations for my next time goal: 3 hours 5 minutes. I planned to run my next marathon in April 2011 in Paris. To register for it, I needed to provide a medical certificate. So I got an appointment with a French physician in Phnom Penh, a man who had a background in sports medicine. When he gave me the results of his tests, he said: "If everyone was as healthy as you, the doctors would be bankrupt!" He was a kind and generous human being. The next year when I returned for another certificate, he graciously provided it free of charge.

I kept training hard in Phnom Penh. I went to bed at 9 every night in order to wake up at 4:45 and get to work. I trained twice a day.

In December, I ran again in the Angkor Wat Half Marathon and got the best time by a Cambodian female. After the race, I was contacted by Satomi, a young woman working for Hearts of Gold, the Japanese NGO that had originally organized the race. Based on the race results, it was going to invite one Cambodian woman and one Cambodian man to run in Japan the following year, she told me. The woman would be me. Would I like to run the Kasumigaura Marathon in March 2011? I accepted, though it meant I would not be able to run in Paris.

But a few weeks before the Japanese race, there was a terrible earthquake and tsunami in Japan. Close to 15,000 people died. The race in Japan was cancelled, and I ended up going to Paris as originally planned.

In that race, I aimed for 3 hours 5 minutes, but I actually ran faster—3 hours 2 minutes. Another 14 minutes off my time! The high-altitude training at HATC that I had finished five months earlier was still enhancing my performance. And with sports gels and white sugar cubes I'd avoided "hitting the wall." I was starting to feel confident that I could get my time below three hours, "breaking the mythical barrier," as marathoners often say.

I contacted Peter to tell him about my achievement. He told me that because I had started training so late in life, my legs were still "young," so to speak. This was why I was able to decrease my running time so much and so fast. Who knew there were advantages to starting a sport late in life?

After the race, I visited Prof. Durosoir at his home in the south of France. He showed me around his big property with its beautiful garden, a fruit orchard and a tennis court. It was a sunny weekend, which included a delicious lunch prepared by his wife at his terrace. His family joined us as well so I was able to meet his two daughters and grandchildren.

I also went to see Prof. Fleury at the University Bordeaux 2. "I taught you to be a good research scientist and now with a PhD what you are going to do with it? Run a marathon!" With his wry smile, he continued. "So, if you ever run at the Olympic Games, that day I will close my lab and without exception all my staff will have to watch the marathon!" We both laughed out loud, as if a deal had been agreed.

#

I felt the best thing for my running career at this point would be to return to Kenya for another round of brutal training. Hearts of Gold had said it would see if it could find me a sponsor, but nothing had come through on that front. So, I contacted the Phnom Penh Post to ask if they would publish an article about my quest. They ran an article the following month, in May, with a picture of me running in Paris. The headline said: "LY Nary looks to sponsors to fund running costs of Olympic dream."

I was daring to eye the next summer Olympics, in London in 2012. But if I could not find a substantial sponsor, I would need to go back to work as a research scientist. I got no response from the newspaper article, so I started to look into job possibilities.

-12-
Out of Money but Not Motivation

One afternoon, I saw a job opening on social media for a lab manager. Chenda Polyclinic, a recruiting firm, was seeking staff for a medical research facility that the U.S. Navy operated in Phnom Penh. Its formal name was Naval Medical Research Unit 2 Phnom Penh, or NAMRU2-PP. It was a sort of competitor of IPC, but was much less open. Its research wasn't readily available to other Cambodian research groups. This was partly because it was a smaller organization, but also because it was military. Some Cambodians, in fact, were convinced that it was doing some other kind of secret research or spying for the U.S. Department of Defense. But I was confident that it had a strictly medical mission. Moreover, I knew they paid their staff better than Institut Pasteur. I quickly updated my CV and sent a short e-mail to them offering my application.

Just as I was heading out for training later that day, my mobile phone rang. It was a woman named Kanya, from Chenda Polyclinic. She was very excited.

She and her husband were recreational runners, and had read about me in the Phnom Penh Post. Kanya thanked God for sending me—she said she hadn't known that someone like me could exist in Cambodia. She had looked for a candidate for the lab manager position for a while, and was becoming resigned to the job going to an expatriate from the United States. She asked me to come for an interview at the organization, known informally as NAMRU, and when I would be available to take the position.

Even though I had very little savings left, I was not quite ready to take the job. I had planned to wait three to six months, still hoping that I might get some sponsorship through the article in the Phnom Penh Post.

But the next morning, after my training, I went in for the interview at NAMRU. Kanya and her husband were there, but so was the director, Capt. William O. Rogers, another American officer, and two Cambodian employees. I was flattered at the turn-out but was honest about how I hoped to find sponsorship in the coming weeks, and if I did, would need to take a long leave to train in Kenya. They suggested a special contract that would let me take unpaid leave when needed for a second training at HATC. They were so kind! It is rare to find jobs where your employer not only allows you to pursue goals outside work, but actually encourages it.

Capt. Rogers requested that, after my laboratory visit, I stop in to see him before I left the building. When I did, he asked that I take the position as it had been posted, and give him six months to petition Navy headquarters in Washington, DC to upgrade the job to a scientific research position. That way, they'd be able to pay me at the correct rank, given my PhD and qualifications.

It was four or five times what IPC was offering me.

I would also be the first Cambodian scientist at NAMRU Phnom Penh.

My apprehensions were fast evaporating. Everyone was enthusiastic and optimistic, and, when I began work, I was given a very warm welcome. No workplace ever made me feel so respected, so confident in my ability. The next week, Chenda Polyclinic gave me a cake for my birthday.

#

Thanks to my new job at NAMRU, I felt fortunate and rich. I sent money to Kenyan runners in Iten, to my foster mother to help make her Christmas with her children and grandchildren more festive, and to my foster sister to cope with some debts she'd run up. I also helped support some Cambodian runners with equipment, products, and occasional cash when they needed it. Things lent to them tended not to be returned, however. I lost a bike and a digital camera this way. This was part of why I stopped running at the National Olympic Stadium. Whenever I went there, I would be listening to people telling me sad stories, and I couldn't concentrate on my training.

However flush I was, I would still need sponsorship to get to Iten for a long training stay of three months, since I would have to take leave without pay. But at least here in Cambodia I had a good job, while the Cambodian runners were barely surviving on their National Athlete allowance.

#

Just after I started at NAMRU, a young Japanese man who was a regional director for Hearts of Gold contacted Bunting and me about possible allowances from Japan. We'd need to have a meeting with the new secretary general of the Khmer Amateur Athletics Federation. Thus began a new experience with the frustrations of dealing with the Cambodian sports bureaucracy.

The secretary general was about 44 and didn't have much experience in sports, despite his position. Bunting and I had to make several attempts to get an appointment. When we finally got one, the man arrived late. The Hearts of Gold representative explained the deal he was offering, and asked the KAAF to issue the administrative papers. But to our surprise, the official gave a little speech saying that Cambodia cared very much for its national athletes, but that all sponsorship allowance should go through the KAAF account before it was provided to us. The Japanese man explained patiently that the allowance was intended for individual athletes, not to sponsor the KAAF. The meeting ended without a clear agreement.

When we were out of the office, Bunting told the Japanese man that if the money went to the KAAF account, we would never see it. In the end, Bunting and I agreed that it would be better if they didn't sponsor us after all.

One day, after four months of work at NAMRU, and seven months after the Kasumigaura marathon's cancellation, Ms. Satomi from Hearts of Gold came to visit me in the lab to announce a possible sponsor for my training in Iten. It was a party in Japan who owned the "AAA Company" in Cambodia. It took a few more weeks for the NGO to arrange a meeting between the owner and me in Phnom Penh. The man did not give me much information about his company, and I couldn't find much on the Internet. It felt a little strange and suspicious.

In the time I'd been working at NAMRU, I hadn't been able to run as much. I wasn't improving like I should have been, because I'd been working long hours to get used to the new work environment with the Navy. I didn't want to take this sponsorship and then betray the donor's trust by not being able to shave the minutes off my marathon time. At the same time, I didn't want to short-change NAMRU in order to run more. I have always thought that if I am doing a job, I should do it properly. NAMRU had treated me very well. I needed to repay them by accomplishing my mission well, so they could be proud of hiring me. This was my own code of honor—it was important to me to give respect when I got it, not to take advantage.

However, there was Bunting, who needed sponsorship for an Iten interlude more than I did. So I suggested to the Japanese company that it should sponsor my running partner instead. At first the company insisted it was me it wanted, but in the end agreed to sponsor both of us.

#

In the meantime, another Japanese company was getting involved in the Cambodian running world. Based in Siem Reap, it operated a tourist business between Japan and Cambodia. One of its shareholders was a comedian who was famous in Japan, Kuniaki Takizaki, known by his stage name Neko Hiroshi.

The company's Cambodian translator contacted Bunting and invited him to a meeting at its hotel in Siem Reap to discuss sponsoring his training. Bunting met with Neko and other company officials, and spent a few nights at their hotel. It was the first time that Bunting had heard about Neko, and he was impressed by the man's fan club. Neko was attended by servants, TV crew, and a Cambodian translator.

The company gave Bunting a new pair of running shoes and $150 cash. They took many pictures of him to post on social media, on Neko's fan page. At the meeting, Bunting learned that Neko was also a long-distance runner, and that he intended to race against Bunting in the upcoming Angkor Wat Half Marathon. Bunting took it that the company wanted him to let Neko beat him, in exchange for the gifts they'd just given him. Clearly they didn't know Bunting very well. He was too proud to let someone else win. He beat Neko in the race.

Soon after, the local English-language newspapers started publishing articles about a controversy involving a Japanese comedian who was applying for Cambodian citizenship and eyeing running in the London Olympic Games, even though he was slower than the country's star long-distance runner, Hem Bunting. That's when we started to realize what Neko was aiming for when he entertained Bunting, and what he was doing with Cambodian sports officials. This disgusting injustice fueled us to train harder and fight back against corruption as best we could. As if a new pair of sneakers and some pocket money would cause Bunting to throw the race!

In January 2012, the KAAF and the NOCC expressed their intention to nominate Neko for the Olympic Games in London, to represent Cambodia. I was enraged. Up until then Neko hadn't won any races in Cambodia against Bunting. Bunting and I were both in Kenya when the news broke, training with sponsorship from AAA to race in April in Paris, where we hoped to set good times and get nominated for the London Olympics. Cambodia was usually quite late nominating its athletes, but this time, it was nominating Neko in February! By deciding so early, officials ensured that Bunting and I wouldn't get the chance to submit our times. It was all very suspicious.

Suddenly, Japanese TV crews were in Phnom Penh following Neko training at the National Olympics Stadium. But not all journalists were buying into Neko's tale. One skeptical Japanese journalist interviewed us, asking if was it true that Neko's company was giving Bunting a monthly salary. This would be good for Neko's image, by showing generosity toward Cambodian athletics. But Bunting clarified that the company hadn't given him anything since their first and last meeting in Siem Reap. Either it had lied about the salary, or someone else had been getting the money all this time.

Bunting had some trouble in these situations because he didn't speak English. I stayed by his side and helped translate for him, trying to prevent him my outspoken friend from saying anything that could get him into trouble. We both had to be careful about how we spoke about the leaders of Cambodia. We stuck to accepted facts: a newly naturalized Cambodian had been selected to represent Cambodia at the Olympics, even though he ran significantly slower than the country's long standing-running champion.

It was well known that many countries sent newly naturalized Kenyans to run for them in the Olympics, to give the country a better chance of winning. This Neko business was the opposite—Cambodian officials didn't seem to care whether he did well for Cambodia. It looked like they just wanted to take the option that would provide them the biggest personal benefit!

However, Neko's nomination had a serious flaw. Under Olympic rules, in order to be eligible to run for Cambodia, Neko would have to have been a Cambodian citizen for at least a year prior to the London games, which were to open in August 2012. I spoke to a Cambodia Daily reporter and asked that the newspaper investigate this point. It published a number of articles. The International Association of Athletics Federations requested his naturalization papers and found out he would only have been a citizen for eight months by the time the London games opened. Because of this, Neko's nomination was withdrawn.

But this did not mean that Bunting would get a nomination for the men's marathon. Officials said he wasn't fit to represent his country because of a "hot temper." I was not nominated either. The KAAF told the Cambodia Daily that at age 40, I was "too old." However, age is not a restriction in the IOC rules. I suspect they didn't select me because I stood by Bunting during the controversy.

I was disgusted. It seemed to me that our Cambodian sports leaders were completely incompetent—selecting athletes for their own petty reasons and their own business, with no thought to the skill of the athletes or Cambodian national pride. I wanted to escape, far from this outrageous society, where money could even buy the honor of your nation!

Every day in Cambodia, you saw or heard about injustice and grief. The poor got poorer and started to grow desperate, because there were no shelters or social protection. The leaders abused their power, and in order to win support, they would pretend to "develop" the country with big-ticket projects that would chase the poor from their houses, and sometimes even burn the houses without mercy!

I felt vulnerable, distressed and angry. It was like my sister had said— you may care about your nation, but your nation doesn't care about you. I worried that if I spent much more time in Cambodia, I would go insane. My emotions were overriding my rational mind. Sometimes I felt the right thing would be to take justice into our own hands and defy the pervasive corruption around us.

One bit of satisfaction we would get out of this whole episode, however, is that we stopped Neko from being wrongfully nominated.

#

After a four-month leave of absence in Kenya, I went back to my job at NAMRU. I kept up my training but started to sustain injuries. I developed serious, painful bursitis in my right hip, which stopped me running for three months. However, in June 2013 I managed to compete in the Phnom Penh Half Marathon, finishing as second woman after a French runner. Bunting was the top Cambodian male.

The UniLab company from the Philippines sponsored that race, and its prize for the first Cambodian male and female runners was an invitation to the Run United Philippines race in Manila that October. UniLab organized the trip for us, paid our expenses, and let us choose to run either a full or half marathon in Manila. I picked the full marathon after studying the results of the previous year's event. I felt I could run in about 3 hours 30 (I still had a residual hip injury) and still have a chance to make the podium. Bunting decided to run the half-marathon.

UniLab took care of us very well during our stay in Manila. A race organizer accompanied us everywhere, gave us tours, and took us food tasting. The best treat for me was sessions at the best physiotherapy clinic in Manila to condition and release the tension from our bodies before the race. It was the first time I'd ever had such a sport treatment.

Bunting and I both came in second in our respective categories, each of us after a Kenyan runner. We made the podium and gave interviews to the newspapers and appeared on the local TV like we were superstars. We won some prize money. Bunting took his money back to Cambodia. My prize was bigger, as it was for a full marathon, so I decided that I was going to use it to travel around the islands of the Philippines.

It wasn't difficult, since so many people spoke English. The weather was warm, like in Cambodia, and the local transport was very affordable. Suddenly, I was free—I could enjoy my recovery time from the marathon. I was travelling alone so I got to choose my own destinations, how I'd get there, and when I went. I hired a personal guide and taxi on one island. On others, I got several hours of massage on the beach. I treated myself to a barbecue dinner at one beach, watching a beautiful sunset along with couples having romantic dinners. At that moment, I felt a little twinge of sorrow at being the only one alone. But the next day was another blissful day. The people there were so friendly as well—I didn't feel at all afraid about being a woman travelling alone.

On Bohol Island, I met some young people training in the hospitality industry at the Harmony Hotel. They were surprised that I was a woman checking into the hotel alone, and they started to ask questions. I told them about my placement in the Manila race the previous Sunday. The students looked me up on the Internet and found me on the Filipino news.

I liked going on morning runs, because the air was fresh, the weather cooler than in Phnom Penh. It was the best way to visit the surroundings and meet local people. After my run and shower, I went to take my breakfast near the pool in the garden, and I could hear the hospitality students murmuring at the back in the bar. Finally, a young boy came to serve me breakfast, and he politely asked permission to ask me questions. "We didn't know that you were a famous Cambodian runner and you are a scientist, with a research doctorate too?" He looked amazed. Then the rest of the students who were watching from the bar joined our conversation, and I got a frenetic company full of curiosity. I had a fantastic time with the students, answering their questions. The conversation took so long that the taxi driver who came to pick me for the day's tour had to wait for me in the lobby. The students asked for photo souvenirs all together near the pool. We are still in contact on social media. Sometimes they repost that photo and recall the good time we had. They send me encouraging messages about my training.

There was also a very nice tuktuk driver who took me around one island. (A tutuk is a carriage pulled by a motorcycle or a small car and is the usual way to travel in Cambodia and the Philippines.) He kept asking me if I was coming back, saying he would wait for me! He took me to the ferry on my last day on that island, and I told him he was very nice, but I couldn't make any promises, so he shouldn't wait. It was nice to be appreciated like that, and it still makes me smile to think about the compliments he gave me.

I was very lucky to have quite good weather during my travels in the Philippines, which are known for their tropical storms. However, as soon as I left, that changed. I departed Luzon island one day before a big storm hit, on October 14, 2013. Typhoon Nari—quite a similar name to mine!—destroyed everything in its path. Bohol Island, which has a unique geological phenomenon called the Chocolate Hills, suffered destruction of several of them in an earthquake after I left. A friend started to joke that it was my fault that everything was destroyed!

During that time, Unilab in Phnom Penh kept in touch with me by email to update us about a press conference that Bunting and I had agreed to give on our return. Now they said it would be better with just me. When I asked why, they said the NOCC was afraid that Bunting would speak up about the controversy with Neko. They knew that whenever the media approached Bunting, he would state his thoughts directly and be indifferent to reprisals, even after losing the London nomination due to his supposed bad temper. However, I appreciated his authenticity and audacity, which was uncommon both in athletes and life in general in present-day Cambodia.

At the end, UniLab got no press conference at all, despite promises from the government that one would be held. The company was quite disappointed and stopped sponsoring the Phnom Penh half marathon. Neko's company stepped in and took over.

I was not surprised by any of this. The hope of building a better Cambodia seemed to diminish every day.

Two years later, I learned that AAA Company, my sponsor in Kenya, had its own ethical problems. The owner was in trouble with the Japanese authorities who accused him of scamming elderly Japanese to invest in dubious or non-existent apartments in Cambodia for their retirement.

#

The Angkor Wat International Half Marathon was the first organized in Cambodia in 1996 by Yuko Arimori, the first Japanese woman to win a marathon medal in the Olympics. It was under Japanese management, and the fee was only $2 for Cambodians. The motto was "Building a better future: Aid for the children and disabled in Cambodia." Since Angkor Wat was a world-renowned heritage site, the race later attracted thousands of foreign runners, who came to run and visit this glorious symbol of Cambodia, the largest religious monument in the world.

Later, Cambodian authorities took over management of the race. The fee skyrocketed to $15 for Cambodians and $75 for foreigners, not including ticket fees for visiting the temples. As of 2017, a one-day pass for a foreigner cost $37. The sponsors technically organized the race and could advertise their brands in the event. This provided potential for further deals with Cambodian sport authorities, who controlled issuance of permits and cashed in the revenues.

As for prize money for runners, the race didn't offer any. This bothered me, as did the practice of putting international and local runners in the same categories, either male or female, with each group having a podium for the top three runners. This made it very difficult for Cambodian runners to get a podium spot. Cambodian runners were still running in second-hand shoes. They struggled every day just to survive. And how could they afford to compete? There was the registration fee, the cost of transportation, food and accommodation for a night or two near the start location, and the risk of being injured. If you made it to the podium, you'd get no prize money but a bag of coupons, a case of beer, and a pair of shoes that didn't fit.

I always wondered why Cambodia wasn't inspired by neighboring countries like the Philippines, Thailand and Singapore. When I had a chance to race in those places, I'd learned they had special rules and rewards to encourage and support local people to compete. There was prize money for the winners, sometimes a reward for the top 10 in each age category! That way, a dedicated athlete from an under-privileged family could have a chance to get out of poverty through sport. The 2017 Angkor Wat race had 10,000 participants, all paying registration fees. A couple of hundred dollars for the Cambodian winners would have been well within the budget.

The Phnom Penh International Half Marathon began in 2010, and it was the first race in the country to award prize money. Local runners were thrilled. They started training hard to win the race. However, every year after that, the prize money kept dropping, while the fees increased! Moreover, local winners learned to check the prize money in the envelope and the bag of goods once they stepped off the podium. Too often, a hundred US dollars would be missing, or the mobile phone prize would be nowhere to be found. If that happened, we had to know immediately, so we could threaten the organizers with telling the local media, in order to pressure them to give us what they had promised.

As every year passed, my heart broke as I witnessed these kinds of injustices. I finally decided not to take part in a system that only increased the gap between rich and poor. I wouldn't pay to run in any of these races, unless I was sponsored to represent Cambodia, and it was free of charge. But not many people followed my views. The races continued to have many paying participants.

Two years after we were denied Olympic nominations, Bunting had completely lost faith that sport might raise people from poverty. He gradually stopped training and ended up leaving Phnom Penh and returning to his family in Stung Treng province.

The following October, in 2014, I flew to Nepal with Megan, a colleague and friend from NAMRU. We were going to go trekking. I had trained a lot for this, loading up a backpack with three kilograms of water, putting on my hiking boots and using the Stairmaster at the gym! I must have looked strange, but I knew that the trek in Nepal would be hard. We had managed to save a little money on our trekking gear, through NAMRU. We asked a favor of one of its Navy officers to use his official mailbox address, and then bought our gear cheaply on Amazon and had it shipped at no cost to the U.S. Embassy in Phnom Penh under his name.

We had decided to go to Manaslu in Nepal, since it was not one of the popular destinations at the time, and we wouldn't encounter too many other tourists. We went in October because the weather was usually good at that time. To bring money into the local economy, the Nepalese government required foreign trekkers to hire a local guide and a porter, so that's what we did.

When we arrived, Megan soon made friends with another trekker couple. They joined us and we ended up going on the trek together, led by two guides and four porters. On the way up, we stayed in very basic country tea houses, for most of the ascent, we didn't have Internet or phone reception.

People in Nepal were very different from people in Southeast Asia, I found. The living conditions and climate are much harsher in the Nepalese mountains, where growing food is itself a challenge. The whole time we were walking, we carried only our backpacks and still found it hard, but the locals were carrying heavy loads up and down the mountain, or working hard in the fields at these altitudes.

It made me reflect on my life and how I had been lucky. At NAMRU, I was paid what I considered to be quite a lot of money, and while I gave the job my best, I didn't feel I worked as hard as these people who lived in the mountains. Yet, I did not have time to truly appreciate the immense and beautiful landscape that magically calmed my tempestuous nature, as I only had limited days of vacation.

I was no longer sure if I wanted to keep working at NAMRU long term. It was good for me to get out of Cambodia, to a place that made me reflect on what I really wanted to make out of my life. This kind of travel reminded me that happiness is not about having a lot of money or power. Of course, you need enough money for a roof over your head and food to eat and healthcare, but after that you can live very simply and overall be happy.

It was lucky that we did not decide to trek on that visit at the famous Annapurna mountain. On October 14, 2014, a severe snowstorm and series of avalanches around Annapurna killed 43 people, including 21 trekkers of various nationalities. Many others were injured and missing.

We only heard about it when we were waiting for clearance to cross the Manaslu pass between two mountain peaks, because the government had declared the path dangerous and forbade crossing due to too much snow. As we were waiting, other groups came down from the mountain and told us that people were stuck at the top in freezing cold and could not cross the pass.

Our base camp had Internet connection, and we found that we had received many, many messages from friends and family who had heard about the tragedy and wanted to know how we were. They hadn't seen our names on the list of the dead, but still they worried. We had been out of connection for the previous few days. Thankfully, we were able to tell them that we were alive and unhurt.

Back in Cambodia, I soon started to feel tense and exhausted, as if I was bleeding inside. Obviously I was not living in harmony with the environment. I felt an urge to get away from that society before it changed me into something else. I had been using the physical pain of pushing myself through running to help me cope with my emotional pain. Step by step, I had become more resigned, and lost my illusions (my faith in good values) in the face of this harsh reality. I was thirsty to be free. I felt attracted to a harmonious place that had wild landscapes, open spaces, peaceful surroundings, and a spiritual life.

But first I would work harder, get the manuscript of my latest research project accepted, and then fly away.

-13-
Tracking Mystery Diseases in Cambodia

When I took the job at NAMRU, it was collaborating with the IPC but not with universities. NAMRU's director, Capt. Rogers, wanted to increase its visibility and foster cooperation with universities and other research groups. So when I first started, I set up a collaboration with a unit at Columbia University to work toward discovery of new pathogens. The overall project was led by the famous Dr. W. Ian Lipkin. In addition to doing pioneering work as a virologist, he had been a science advisor on the famous movie "Contagion," which dramatized the spread of a dangerous pathogen and the world's reaction to it.

On my side of the project, NAMRU was conducting a surveillance study of unidentified respiratory infections in Cambodia. Cambodians suffering such symptoms as severe vomiting and nausea, coughing, aches and pains, and other possible indicators of a respiratory tract infection would be screened by doctors to rule out severe and contagious illnesses such as malaria, dengue fever and influenza. If they didn't have any of those pathogens, they would go on to another screening, which tested for other pathogens. If the samples made it through all this screenings without being identified, they were classified as "Negative, but with severe symptoms." They were then stored away.

To identify the infectious agents that could be responsible for these diseases, we had to look back through more than ten years' worth of clusters of these "negative but with severe symptoms" cases—that is, any time in which a group of more than five persons had come to the same health center within a short period of time to look for help with their symptoms. We tested these clusters to see if common known pathogens had occurred, and especially if there were any re-emerging pathogens, such as polio or poxvirus. If the samples still came out negative, we would look for possible new pathogens.

During this time I also taught immunology to third-year students in the Faculty of Pharmacy at the University of Health and Science in Phnom Penh. This was part of an attempt to strengthen the connection between the U.S. Navy and Cambodia's National University.

I loved teaching. It brought me joy to see the younger generation learning and progressing. Many students were smart, hard workers. They were honest and innocent and earnest—it was like I was seeing myself again at their age, with a heart full of hope for a better future. It was an honor to be their lecturer—they offered me such warm friendship! I created a Facebook Immunology group for them to share questions and documents from class, but I had to tell them that I couldn't accept any Facebook friend requests, to avoid accusations of favoritism or corruption regarding exams and marks.

I thought a lot about NAMRU's aim to be more open to the public. There were still many people who saw the group not as a scientific institution but as a secret defense force or a U.S. intelligence agency sent to spy on Cambodia. I have always thought that sharing knowledge and expertise was a worthy goal in itself, but doing so would also serve to expel these false images. Eventually, I talked to Dr. Rogers about starting a scientific seminar, to include our colleagues from the Institut Pasteur. A conference, I reasoned, would be a place where everyone could share ideas and projects freely.

Dr. Rogers thought this was an excellent idea. Not only that, he wanted to use the conference to invite outside visitors to give talks, to show that we were open and transparent, and that we had nothing to hide. We held the conference at the National Institute of Public Health.

To improve the wellbeing and motivation of the NAMRU local staff, I also set up a running team, and found sponsors for the team to race in Siem Reap at the Angkor Wat Inter Half Marathon.

#

When I started on my journey of rediscovering my heritage, I went to Cambodia with the intention of spending a year living there doing what I could to help in the country's recover. But now I had been back in Cambodia on and off for over 20 years, and things had started to get more and more bleak. Instead of the place I remembered, Cambodia seemed to have become more and more corrupt.

I like to think well of people, but I couldn't have any sympathy for those who were ready to make vile compromises to get ahead in life. I never wanted to cause trouble, but I felt I had to stand up against the attitude of "going with the flow." It facilitated so much corruption. I saw many people be disloyal or abuse their positions, causing problems for the people they exploited. Sometimes it seemed like everyone, except me, was trying to get ahead with no thought for others.

Everywhere there was evidence of corruption. For example, when someone works for a private company in Cambodia, the company holds back 5-20 percent of salary for taxes, depending on how much is earned. All countries take taxes from their people, but in most taxes go towards helping the government care for its citizens! In Cambodia, there are no social security services, such as unemployment insurance, public health insurance and almost no effort by the government to improve the public infrastructure. So where is the tax money going?

While I loved my time teaching, I found myself holding back from telling my students about my general disillusionment. I wanted them to keep believing that hard work, honesty and determination would make them successful and change our society. Some of them, I knew, had already encountered the kind of corruption that I was aware of. Several were at the university on scholarships from the French Foundation and had grown up in rural areas, where the misuse of public funds was particularly bad, as evidenced by the very few functioning public services in health and education. It was heartbreaking to look at the students and know that despite everything I said, they would probably have to pay corruption money if they were going to get a job in any public institute.

I was also finding that I wasn't suited for working in a military organization. Every day that passed in the office in Phnom Penh, I felt my mind numbing from the routine. I had to be at the office from 7 a.m. to 4 p.m., even if I didn't have much to do. I logged in and out with a fingerprint every day, and if I was late three times in a month, there were penalties. There were cameras in every office and every corner of the office. It was only in the bathroom that we had any privacy!

This was very different from Mount Sinai, where researchers were autonomous and responsible for their own research schedules in order to make their research maximally productive. I felt it was a waste of time having to be at work if I didn't have anything to do, then having to ask for special authorization to stay late at the office or to come in on the weekend when there was a big project to finish. I could have used that time so much better—I could have been training, or catching up on my sleep or any number of things.

But this was the military way of life. There was no freedom to follow your creativity, or research what was interesting. Everything, every equipment order, every request for research, had to be passed through the chain of command.

In addition, leadership was changing all the time. During my three and a half years at NAMRU, I worked under three directors and six commanding officers. Most of the Americans spent at most two years at the organization. Different directors had different ways of doing things.

#

In November 2012, I was in Yangon, Myanmar, with a few hours to spend before taking an airplane to Cambodia.

In front of a park, a fortune teller read my palm. I was told, for the second time, that I was going to die young! It was another wake-up call. I was forced again to ponder the definition of "young." By this point I was over forty. I had seen many loved ones get sick, and several of them die.

Just like the first time I had had my palm read, I was reminded that I had to live listening to my heart. I had to set my own boundaries, and be brave, authentic, and loyal, and go against the flow if I felt it was going in a wrong direction. So I re-checked my priorities. I realized that what was all-important to me was to be capable of running a marathon and breaking the mythical barrier of three hours. To do that, I would need extensive time to myself. It was time to move on from NAMRU. It was no easy decision to leave research. But I could see no other way.

But before I could leave the job, I had to finish my collaboration with Dr. Lipkin at CII. I scurried to bring together the final research results. The pressure was amplified by that fact that someone influential seemed to want to receive formal credit in the final paper without having taken part in the research. I steeled myself and with a series of meetings and carefully crafted emails, I successfully objected. Once it was over, I was glad to have stood my ground.

Soon after, we submitted the manuscript. I felt freed—glowing and joyous!

The manuscript was accepted by the *Virology Journal* only a few weeks later. I was grateful to Dr. Lipkin and his team for their collaboration.

Before I left Cambodia, I had one last thing that I wanted to do to be sure that I had done all I could concerning medicine in the country. I knew that if I left without at least trying to set up a collaborative research partnership, I would regret it. So I started to investigate the feasibility of a collaboration between CII, IPC and a Cambodian institution. I had already been offered an opportunity to set up a collaboration project with CII, which would be a great chance to have the United States fund the research. Now I obtained an informal meeting with the director of IPC—we had known each other since 2000, when I was a student in Paris and he was one of my professors. I was excited. I explained my idea for a collaboration between the three partners, and that IPC could be the one to provide the local experience and lend some of its equipment. I expected encouragement, perhaps advice, but he told me that I was being unrealistic. It was a utopian dream, he said. French and U.S. scientists wouldn't collaborate; there was too much mistrust and resentment between them. I was disappointed, but at least I could hand in my resignation with no regrets, knowing that I had tried.

With that settled, I was suddenly able to focus on a new life. My foster mother and some friends of hers were coming to Cambodia, and now I could take them to see the sights. I could visualize all the open time I would have, and how happy I would be.

Of course, many of my friends and family could not understand how I could walk away from an important, well-paying job in research. But looking back, I know I made the right decision. I was going to be the person I wanted to be instead of the person that everyone expected me to be.

When I quit, I had worked for the Navy for three and a half years. I didn't have another job to go to. I just had my savings and the goal of shaving two more minutes off my marathon time, to get it under three hours.

-14-
A Last Attempt at My Running Goals

At the end of November 2014, the third annual Global Limits race was to take place in Cambodia. It would have six stages conducted on six successive days. Racers would run a total of 220 kilometers, with distances getting longer day by day—30 or 35 kilometers on the first day increasing until the fourth day to 62 kilometers. All the runners' belongings and food would be transported by car from site to site. At the end of each day, runners would sleep in tents or local houses.

The event could take a maximum of 65 runners but this year only 43 had signed up. Most were not professionals, but enthusiasts from developed countries who were able to afford the event's rather high fees. The opening and awards ceremonies were to be held in fancy hotels, with beautiful receptions.

I'd already decided that I wouldn't participate. First, I considered the fee to be exorbitant, considering I'd be running in my own country, and I already knew most of the areas. Second, it was a tremendous distance to be running, especially with the injured hip that I was still nursing. Two hundred twenty kilometers in six stages, sleeping in tents, eating dried food and sometimes going without showers—to me it was too extreme. Also, it was just a week before maman was coming, so I wanted to stay at home to make sure everything was ready for her.

A few days before the race was scheduled to start, Stefan, the director of the race, and Manu, the course director from Spain, were in Phnom Penh to prepare and check the course markers and other details. They suggested I should meet with them, as I was interested in their multiple-stage race in Bhutan.

Stefan made a pitch to me: he wanted me to run the Cambodia Global Limits because an accomplished local runner would be good for the event. Having me would help educate the other runners on the local culture and history. Over and over, he urged me to join the race; I kept politely declining.

I did manage to get them to talk a bit about the Bhutan race, because I needed some advice about it. In Cambodia, the terrain is flat. My training at high altitudes in Kenya had hills, but I didn't have to run up and down steep trails. I had no experience in the kind of mountainous environment I would find in Bhutan. The thought of running up and down rocky cliffs through a beautiful landscape of forests, villages and mystic monuments gave me excited chills, but I couldn't risk dying or getting hurt because of inexperience. I would need some minimum training to survive.

Stefan ended our long meeting by asking me whether I was available on Friday, November 28 to attend Global Limits' opening ceremony. That was my last day at work for NAMRU. He persisted—what about after work? He told me I should come so I could talk to people there who had run in Bhutan.

I finally agreed.

#

That Friday, I conducted my last field work in a province outside the city, then rushed home to shower and dress up a little for the ceremony.

The opening buffet dinner was in the garden of the four-star Himawari Hotel with a view of the Mekong River. When I arrived, Stefan was waiting in a big armchair in the hotel lobby to welcome the runners. Manu was standing nearby chatting joyfully in Spanish with a European friend. Manu introduced us. His friend was named Salva. A smiling, shaved-head and rather small man, he exuded peacefulness. He was also an expert on mountain races, with more than thirty three years of experience.

We stood aside and started talking. I asked many naïve questions about Bhutan, how to train for it and what food to bring for a multiple-stage race. Salva asked about my current running program and the food supplements I used. It was all very technical.

Once all the runners had arrived and taken their seats, Stefan grabbed a microphone to give a welcome speech. I saw myself as just a guest, or more like an observer at a new kind of sport event. But then Stefan announced that there were two special persons present whom he would like to introduce. One was Chanthy, the first Cambodian female ever to take part in the event. She would run with her uncle Vannarin, who had run last year. The room gave her a big cheer.

Then Stefan turned my way to make his second introduction. "Nary!" He called me the famous female Cambodian marathoner. He praised my running accomplishments, then announced to the room that I was planning to make it to the Olympics to represent Cambodia!

I had entrusted him with that secret when I met him with Manu. If I had known he would spill it out here, I would never have told him. The runners applauded, long and loud. I was so uncomfortable—I wished I could run away and hide.

Then, right there in front of everyone, he asked if I would change my mind and run with them.

Instantly, everyone was making a fuss over me. One of the runners started shouting my name. In the atmosphere of camaraderie, more people joined in.

"Don't worry if you haven't trained! I'm going to walk!"

"Don't worry if you don't have protein recovery, or electrolytes, or gels! I brought so much with me! You can have some of mine!"

I wanted to disappear under the table, but at the same time I felt very touched to receive this warm and loving comradeship. The pressure was all good-natured; they genuinely wanted me to take part.

I said "yes" just to quiet them all down. Now everyone cheered louder, as if they had just won a victory. I was already feeling nervous. I was panicking at the thought that I had only eleven hours until the race would start. I hadn't prepared anything; I had bought no dried food. I started to rebuke myself—it was stupid and crazy to make a last-minute decision. I wondered if I would die from the big event, or injure myself badly.

But there was no turning back. After the speeches, Stefan gave me quick instructions—the race rules and the schedule for the next day. I would need to arrive at the Himawari Hotel at 9 a.m. to drop my bag off and catch the bus that would take all the runners to a pagoda at Kampong Thom province where the race would begin on Sunday. I would have to get a medical check, fill out documents, and sign medical waivers. He gave me a list of mandatory equipment, and asked a couple of the volunteers to help me collect everything I would need. I was so tense I could hardly enjoy the buffet.

I told Stefan very clearly that I still wasn't sure if I was going to actually run the race. If I didn't show up at the hotel the next morning, he should assume I wasn't coming, and send off the bus without me.

The rest of the evening was frantic. I rushed home and began to pack quickly with the help of my housekeeper, making sure that my luggage didn't exceed the weight limit of 10 kilograms. By the time I finished, it was 1:00 a.m. I texted one or two friends to tell them where I was going, and when I should be home, just in case something happened to me. I laid down, but did not sleep much or well. The pessimistic side of my mind just wouldn't stop worrying. I tried to fight back by reassuring myself that the race was in my own country. I spoke the language, and if I decided to quit, I could easily catch a bus home.

I woke up early and couldn't eat breakfast. I rushed to the supermarket as soon as it opened at seven to buy the food I would need, then rushed to the hotel to catch the bus to the first stage.

#

When we arrived at the starting site camp in Kompong Thom, I learned that my registration fee had been waived. All I had to do was check my equipment and get all my documents filled out and signed. That was all good for me. I was now determined to use this event as the start of my training for my next marathon and the future race in Bhutan.

The Spanish guy Salva was looking out for me. He gave me salt pills to prevent dehydration, telling me to take one every hour. He said he would wait for me at the end of each stage with recovery protein, which I should take within thirty minutes. I tried to remember all the instructions. I would follow them like a lab protocol.

I learned later that at first Salva hadn't thought much of my running ability, especially when I told him my training schedule. It didn't seem like a lot for someone who wanted to be in the Olympics. At the hotel that night, I seemed to him more like a yogi than an ultra trail runner, with my thin body in a simple but elegant white cotton t-shirt, loose white linen trousers and long, soft Nepali scarf with a warm color gradient of yellow, orange and red.

Two friends of Salva were at the race: Manu and Pepe, who was a checkpoint volunteer. They had going a sort of boy's game before the race started: They would bet on which women would be the top three. Since talking to Stefan, Manu knew that my best time at the marathon was close to three hours, so he considered me one of the most likely to be on the podium. Salva, on the other hand, dismissed this, and said that since I didn't train much, I wouldn't even finish the first stage.

That Saturday evening, we had to sleep all together on the ground inside the pagoda under individual pink mosquito nets set side by side. The pagoda architecture amplified all the noises the runners made— every snore and cough and whispered remark. The toilet cabin was three hundred meters from the pagoda through absolute darkness. I had a habit of going to the bathroom at least once a night, so I had to use the headlamp that someone lent me for the race.

That first night was terrible. I couldn't sleep because of the constant noise and snoring, and the heavy heat and humidity. Even though all the windows of the pagoda were open, no air was circulating. I didn't have an inflatable mattress or a mat to soften the ground; every position I tried on the hard floor hurt.

Sunday morning, at the starting line of the first stage, we had a blessing ceremony from the local monks. I wore a huge, floppy cotton hat, to protect my face from the sun. This confirmed Salva's judgment that I was not a professional runner. To him, I looked like I was going to the beach.

I planned to use this event to mark my return to serious marathon training. On the first stage, I started off slow, with the back group. While I jogged, I took the time to chat with some of the other slow runners. Then, I started catching up with some of the front runners who were slowing down, some with stomach problems. I picked up my pace and started passing more runners.

Later Salva told me that when he saw me coming toward the stage one finish line with my big hat on, talking to people and smiling, he began to have respect for me as a runner. I was the second female and fourth overall.

After the run, I joined Salva to collect my promised protein recovery. Then I took a bath with bucket and scoop, picked up my ten-kilogram bag, and selected my sleeping spot. At stage two, the camp was set in two traditional wooden stilt Khmer houses. The mosquito nets were put up in the big common area of the first floor, while under the houses animals like chickens, pigs and cows were kept. In the back yard, there were big jars full of rainwater.

Later, I prepared my dried-food dinner and went to socialize with the runners and local people. I couldn't help noticing that Salva was discreetly observing my every move. Late the evening, he approached and told me that he arranged with the Cambodian site manager to move his mosquito net to the stilt house on the opposite side of the road in order to escape the snoring and get a better night's sleep. Did I want to join him? That sounded like a great idea, as now I had not slept well for two nights. Salva told me how to proceed and not to let Stefan know.

My net was moved. Salva's friends Pepe and Manu came by and joked with him in Spanish. When it came time to go to sleep, Salva kept asking me questions. I politely answered, though I wished he would stop talking and let me get some sleep!

For the rest of the stages, Pepe and Manu joked in Spanish with Salva whenever they could. I suspected they were talking about me. Salva always seemed to have his eyes on me, and he was always smiling. Was he some sort of psychopath, or did he have true tender feelings for me?

#

The stage two finish was at the great Twelfth Century temple Preah Khan in Angkor near Siem Reap. Salva was the second male and I was second female. Christine, an Austrian, was third female.

At this point, and until the end of the overall race, we had to share a small tent with another runner of our choice. I had originally arranged to be in a tent with Christine.

That day was my Cambodian runner friend Vannarin's birthday, and he suggested taking Chanthy, me and some Cambodian staff to go to celebrate his birthday with wild pig soup and roasted chicken at a nearby village. But before that, he would ask a staff member to drive us to take a bath in a small lake. Of course we had to sneak out to do this, getting away from Stefan after he had given the evening briefing. We kept our plan secret from the other runners, because we were all supposed to be under the same rules, getting only three liters of water for our shower and drinking, and making our dinner with hot water they provided—and nothing else.

Just before leaving the camp site for the birthday dinner, I noticed Stefan, Manu, Pepe and Salva talking in the middle of the camp site. There seemed to be some issue about tents.

When I came back from the birthday dinner, Christine told me she had moved out and was sharing a tent with a German racer named Mickael. I was a bit surprised but didn't really mind. I would have the whole tent to myself. They were a bit small for two people, so I felt lucky.

As I was setting up my sleeping space in my tent, I was very surprised when Salva showed up, asking if he could share. It turned out that the tent issue he had been discussing with his friends was this: Salva's tent had been stolen.

It would be a bit embarrassing to share a tent with a man, but I had gotten into the event for free, and Salva had been very helpful so far, giving me his salts and his protein, and being very friendly. So I didn't feel I could say no.

I let him in and resettled my belongings back to the far corner of the tent, leaving the most space possible between him and me, so he couldn't misinterpret anything.

It was awkward. Salva at first thought I was a prude—I wasn't like the female runners he had known before. The other women had been used to living in close quarters like this, and had gotten used to undressing in front of people. They would just take their bras off and change in front of men and not care. But because of my upbringing, I was far too modest for that. I changed with my back to Salva and a blanket wrapped around me so that I didn't show anything.

Salva remained very attentive to me. He noticed I didn't have a sleeping pad. He offered to give me one of his mattresses. I refused at first because I didn't want to take advantage of him, but then gave in.

We went to sleep. Now everybody thought we were a couple.

We finished the fourth stage at the Phnom Kulen waterfalls. So far, we had run 160 kilometers and my body was starting to suffer. My leg muscles felt heavier and cramped up. I had to massage them seriously at night. Salva offered me some ointment, and then offered to do the massage for me. But I felt awkward at the idea of him touching my body. I told him that I was big enough to do it myself.

"But you're doing it wrong!" he told me.

"So tell me how to do it and I'll do it myself!" I grabbed the pouch of ointment from his hands.

That night, I bought a can of beer, hoping that it would help me get to sleep faster. I had been sleep-deprived for many days. I offered to share it with Salva, and was surprised by his answer—he didn't drink alcohol. I wondered if that was a religious belief. Not at all, he just didn't like alcoholic drinks.

Every night Salva seemed to have endless energy. He kept on asking questions and making jokes like "Are all men in Cambodia blind?" He asked this because I was single at the time. He kept starting new conversations when all I wanted was to relax my body in silence and go to sleep!

That evening, I was approached by Laura, a volunteer I knew who was part of the running community in Phnom Penh. She asked me if, on the night of the award ceremony in Siem Reap, I wouldn't mind sharing a hotel room with Salva. Because I'd entered the race so late, Stefan hadn't planned a room for me. I was quite surprised that she'd feel she had to ask, as we were now used to sharing a tent where any privacy was impossible. It didn't matter to me, but Salva was the VIP guest, and it was his decision. I suggested to Laura that I could get a guest house near the hotel. But Laura kept up with the idea of us sharing, saying that Salva looked like a nice and gentle guy, always smiling and caring. Then she said Stefan would like to see some romance in the event. That was certainly strange! She went to report my answer to Stefan. He asked

Salva about the arrangement and of course Salva was more than happy to share his room with me.

We finished the sixth and last stage in front of Angkor Wat temple in Siem Reap after running past various other temples in the complex. I had not only finished all the stages, but had ended on the podium as third overall female. I could have been second, but on the fifth stage, I got lost on the path and felt so discouraged that I finished the race walking instead of running. Salva came in second.

We finally got to our room at the 5-star hotel, and our grand dating adventure began. It has continued to this day.

#

I told Salva that my secret aim behind resigning my job at the Navy facility was to try to run a marathon under three hours, and my further goal was to inspire the young generation, especially Cambodian females, to excel in sport and academia.

He offered to be my coach. He used to run a marathon in 2 hours 28. He had also once wanted to be an Olympian, but it didn't happen, so he started practicing different extreme sports, from canoeing in wild rivers, to trail skiing and paragliding, but running in the mountains was his major focus. He was competing not only at the national level in mountain running, where in different races he had come in second and third in the Spanish championship, but on different continents. Basically he took part in all the famous races in the world. In fact, he had become one of the legends in short, medium and ultra-long trail disciplines.

But now, at this point of his life, he felt he didn't need to prove anything, and he would have time to help me. If I came to Léon, his home in Spain, with him, he could train me to achieve my under-three-hour goal. He had a day job as an informatics programmer for the Spanish social security system, but he finished work at 2:30 p.m. every day. He could train me in the afternoons and on weekends. As for my hip injury, he said he knew the best physiotherapist in León—I could go to him and get it professionally treated.

I agreed. I had already saved up some money intending to go back to Kenya. Now I would spend it on going to Spain.

#

Salva had fallen in love with me quite early on, but it took me longer, but not much. By the time we reached the end of the race, though, he and I had gotten much closer.

I appreciated that he didn't snore, that his feet didn't smell bad, that he didn't drink alcohol, and that he could run faster than me. I was surprised by his age, as he was with mine. Salva thought I was in my early 30s, while I thought he was an old man. Since he ran in a lot of different countries, under diverse climates without taking good care of his skin, he appeared to be in his 60s because of the wrinkles on his skinny face. I was surprised to learn that he didn't have any children, and that he was only about 10 years older than I was.

Salva had never had a serious long-term girlfriend. Thirteen months was the longest a relationship had ever lasted. His family and friends were always joking about him being a bachelor forever. He had never found "the other half of his orange," as the Spanish expression goes. Having a family was not his priority—most of his free time was dedicated to his extreme sports. Nevertheless, he appeared simple, sincere and dedicated to making our relationship work. Still, it was a little frightening for me at first. He said such grand things about me—I was sure he couldn't really mean them.

He had planned to stay for a few days in Siem Reap after the race, but I had to get back to Phnom Penh to collect maman and her two friends from the airport. He said he'd cancel his Siem Reap stay and follow me to Phnom Penh. Don't, I said. I won't have time for you because my mother is arriving. I left on a bus; Salva, not to be deterred, would stay behind to cancel arrangements for his extended stay in Siem Reap, then get to Phnom Penh as quickly as he could.

My whole bus ride he was texting me declaring his love for me. With that, things began to move exceptionally quickly between us.

He found a flight to Phnom Penh. He arrived at the airport just before maman and her friends and I drove them all back to my house. My car was a small Toyota Camry, and it was hard to fit five people and all the luggage in.

At first, I introduced Salva to maman as a friend whom I'd met at the race. I didn't want to shock her. She might think I was sleeping with a man I'd only known for a week!

On one of the evenings, I organized a barbeque dinner on a boat on the Mekong. I invited my Cambodian family, so that my French mother could finally meet them and get to know them. I invited Salva mostly to be polite. I had expected him to say, "No, that's all right—it's an event for you and your family." But he said yes, and so I had to introduce him not only to my French mother but my Cambodian family in Phnom Penh.

But he got along very well with everyone, including maman. In the end, I did tell her I was dating Salva. I explained that I hadn't known him very long, but that he was a good person, and that I wanted to give it a try. She agreed with me—she had talked to him and liked him.

Once Salva returned to Spain, he told his own family about me. Usually, after his races, his sisters called him for news about his adventures. They especially wanted to know if he got on the podium. This time, Salva told them, "I got better than a trophy!" They were intrigued, and a little stunned, because they had never expected Salva to find a girlfriend. But they were also very happy and excited for him.

Maman's visit was a joy. I took her and her friends to see all the main sights of Cambodia. It was a very busy 20 days, but I made sure to give them time to rest. At the end, she told me she had had such a good time. She was especially glad to meet my Cambodian family, and finally see the people she'd been told about and who had been such a big part of my life. As for Salva, she told him to be nice to me.

Two days after she left, I flew to Spain to discover a new country with its culture, language, food, and terrain for training. And to see if things really would work out long-term with Salva.

—Part Six—

Inspiring the Next Generation

-15-
A Marathon in Under 3 Hours

That year, I spent Christmas with Salva and his family. This was a surprise to his family, and not just because of me. For the previous 15 years, Salva had spent Christmas alone in a mountain retreat (he didn't care much for the traditional ways of celebration) and then gone to visit his family the following day. This year, with me to introduce, he had broken that pattern. His family was excited to have him on the big day itself, especially since his parents were old, and his mother's health had been declining for the past 10 years. Sadly, she passed away four months later.

I had arrived at Madrid Airport on Christmas Eve. Salva was waiting there for me. After three and a half hours of driving, we arrived in the city where he lived, León, just in time to dress up for Christmas dinner at his parents' apartment in Astorga town 40 minutes away.

León used to be the capital of the Kingdom of León. It is located on a plateau about 850 meters above sea level in northwest Spain, surrounded by mountains that reach up to 2,000 meters. It is quite a small city, with only 130,000 people, but it has a fabulous historical and architectural heritage. It's on the famous Camino de Santiago, a UNESCO World Heritage site and a well known tourist and pilgrimage destination.

Snow was of course unheard-of in Cambodia, but I had seen it occasionally when I lived in Paris and New York, though it was not very deep and got dirty quickly. Not here. Arriving in León that Christmas Eve, I beheld a sight I had never seen before: snow that was deep, soft, and fresh on the ground, pristine, the sun shining on it, making it sparkle and gleam around me. The pine trees were bent under the heavy snow, providing a fairy atmosphere of immense, quiet nature.

In the days after Christmas, Salva was very attentive. Having brought me to Spain, he wanted to show me the best of everything to convince me that his country was the place I should live. He had limited time to win me over—I'd arrived on an air ticket with a return flight three weeks later. He wanted to make me happy and glad that I had come to see him. But I had come to train, of course, so we got right down to work. We started running.

For the previous 20 years, I had lived in busy cities, where the only animals were birds and pets. Here, there was wildlife all around. Salva's apartment was only two kilometers from a forest, and when we went running there, we often saw storks, foxes, deer, eagles, wild boars, snakes and rabbits in our path.

There were farm animals all over the place, too—flocks of sheep and herds of cows. I felt like Heidi, the little mountain girl under her grandfather's care in the Swiss Alps, arriving in a new place and feeling awe at the new sights. Sometimes, I paused in my running to take a deep breath and embrace the beauty of the nature, but not very often, as I didn't want to get my taskmaster Salva annoyed! He knew all the paths, and where to get drinking water in a fountain or directly from a spring in the mountains. I could point to any of the mountains in the area, even the smallest peaks, and he could tell me their names. I felt so lucky and grateful to have met Salva.

In León, I became aware how famous Salva was as one of the first Spanish trail and mountain runners. It wasn't unusual for people to stop him on the street and ask to take a photograph with him. He was often asked to give interviews, attend conferences, oversee training camps and receive tributes from towns. He appeared regularly on TV sports channels. He had not only competed in the most famous, challenging and toughest races on all continents (including "Transvulcania," "Marathon des Sables" and "The Jungle Ultra Marathon") and in all climate conditions—he had won most of them.

When I started to meet people in the running community in León, I immediately felt the closeness of our shared passion. There were runners of different age groups, some older than me, and we all enjoyed the well-being brought about by an active lifestyle.

Food was another reason I liked this place. It was very affordable, especially fresh vegetables, fruit, meat and seafood. I could buy half a kilo of strawberries for one euro! Salva used to say it was dangerous to go shopping with me because I wanted to buy everything and try cooking new things.

León is also famous for its *embutidos*—a type of cured meat sausage— and for cheese. One day I met Tomás, the mayor of the town of Posada de Valdeón, in the Picos de Europa mountains, who was a friend of Salva's. Tomás was pleased to lead me on a personal tour of one of his famous cheese factories. The cheeses made there are internationally famous and are exported to different continents. Recently, Posada de Valdeón had been named as making best blue cheese in the world! Tomás answered all my questions, and at the end of the visit, he generously gave me a big bag full of cheese samples to try at home.

Further up the mountain lay Peñalba de Santiago, a place of holiday houses and family homes but few fulltime inhabitants. It is one of the most beautiful villages in Spain, boasting views of Valle del Silencio and Aquilianos mountain. Set in a virgin valley dominated by leafy oak forest, rivers and natural waterfalls, it felt like a throwback to medieval times. Cars are not allowed to enter the town other than to unload. It's incredibly well cared for and restored. The church of Santiago, of pure Mozarabic style, stands in the middle (I first saw it covered by a white snow mantle) and is an official national monument.

The peace I found in Spain was just what I was looking for. I could not imagine a greater contrast with Phnom Penh, with its traffic jams and reckless drivers, constant din of construction, and repressive politics. Here, in Spain, all was tranquil and beautiful. I felt like an enchanted child, finally in a place where she really belonged.

When the three-week mark of my stay came around, I extended. León was clearly the perfect place for a good training regimen. Salva's wooing was having its effects too, and before long I realized I wanted to make my home with him.

#

But to return to the subject of training, that soon dominated my stay. For the first time, I didn't need to earn money while I trained, so I did it with particular intensity. Generally I trained twice a day, seven days a week, all the time keeping my mind on my goal of getting my marathon time under three hours. In the morning, I trained alone while Salva was at the office. In the afternoons, I ran with Salva or linked up with a local organization, the Intelligent Interval running club, which held training sessions in the evenings twice a week.

I made frequent discoveries when I went off by myself. Once, while passing through hilly fields near San Andres, I came across some isolated, unfamiliar domes in the land. They looked like secret war bunkers. But I found out that they were actually underground bodega cellars where families kept their wine. The Bierzo area had been named the best wine destination on the planet. The families stored wine in underground cellars while it aged, to keep it at a constant temperature, and now those cellars dotted the landscape.

When I ran alone, sometimes I came upon flocks of hundreds of sheep. If I could see the shepherd, I would call greetings to him and carefully walk through the herd. I did my best to avoid the area's huge Spanish Mastiff (or mastín) dogs.

One day, I was running alone down a small path partly covered in snow. I was going quite fast when I reached an open barn. Suddenly, a terrible barking surprised me in mid-stride. I started to turn back, but it was too late. Four gigantic mastíns surrounded me! I was hopeless and desperate, not seeing any owners nearby. I thought that these gigantic livestock guardians would eat me in one bite! Timidly, I showed them my empty hands, and pronounced a few Spanish words to show them I was friendly. Their barking turned less aggressive, and slowly I stepped backwards, not daring to turn around and run until I was far enough away. I never went down that path again.

#

Salva initiated me to a type of running that couldn't be more different than what I was used to: winter mountain running. On many weekends, we spent five or six hours training in the mountains, running up and down from one summit to another until we reached the highest one.

We were running through snow, frozen slippery areas and on stony mountain slopes. This scared me at first. I tried my best to dominate my fear and not show how unsettled I was, while at the same time recalling Salva's instructions: "On the unstable stone, you have to jump quickly from one to another, otherwise the stone could slide under your weight, and you with it."

That was easy for him to say, with his 34 years of trail running experience! I always felt like I needed a few seconds to plan my next step before jumping. My inner voice was always warning me not to go too fast, in case I couldn't stop or took a curve too fast. I started to wonder—if I fell over a mountain cliff, would I die, or just be horribly injured? Would it be better to die than to be awfully disabled by the fall?

Salva enjoyed watching me run in the technical parts, providing advice here and there. He nicknamed me *Patito*, meaning duckling, because of the way I went down slopes.

But getting to the top of a mountain made it all worthwhile. The view from the highest peak in the area was absolutely magnificent: an immense ocean of clouds under our feet. A blue spot far below was the lake, and small villages could be seen in the valleys. During the winter we could not stay long because it was so windy and cold. We were only able to take a few pictures of each other before we had to go back down.

On these outings we ran wrapped up in warm clothes and thick socks. They were soon soaked with sweat. We had to keep going— if we stopped with so much moisture so close to our skin, it would freeze. After every run like this, we changed into dry clothes we kept in the car to avoid getting sick. At times like those, I could think that Salva was completely insane. Nothing stopped him from running. And of course, I could hear my inner voice telling me I was just as stupid, for always following him. But wonderfully, and surprisingly, every time we ended up alive.

On the way back, I would often fall asleep in the car and wake up with a stiff neck and drool on my chin. I got in bed around 10 p.m., which was when most Spanish people start having their dinner, and fell dead asleep within seconds. Often, I had the feeling that I might not wake up the next day. But sometimes I thought that if I died right then I would be happy. But it would be better not to—I still wanted to know if I could reach my goal of running a marathon in under three hours.

Back at his apartment, we grew increasingly comfortable with each other. When I first met Salva, I was concerned that he might be lying to me about himself. Perhaps he had a complicated past, with kids at home whom I might have to look after. He was older than me—it wasn't out of the question. But those fears proved completely unfounded. Salva was everything he claimed to be.

Cooking was one of the many things that brought us close together. He said that I had had a very lax training regime before, and now he might have to do all the cooking, to give me the time I'd need. However, I surprised him about that. In my many years living alone, I had become a decent cook. I made him my culinary assistant. I would give him a shopping list and he would buy all the ingredients during his office break. In the kitchen, he would help me closely. Sometimes the utensils I was using and had laid aside nearby disappeared because Salva had whisked them away and washed them. We'd have a good laugh. I realized I had to be careful around the cleaning cyclone!

I enjoy cooking when I have enough time. It's relaxing. I feel like I'm in a laboratory experimenting when I adapt a recipe, then play with different flavors. Usually, my dishes are colorful: green, white, red, orange, yellow and purple. The good thing about Salva is that he's not a foodie. Even when my dishes did not turn out quite how I wanted, they were delicious to him!

Partially because we were training so hard, I ate quite a lot. At first I felt a little embarrassed about it, but Salva told me that he loved that about me. He was glad that I was the sort of person who enjoyed food, not like some other women who would eat only a salad leaf at meals, because they were obsessed with how they looked, not with enjoying their lives.

Salva was always showering me with compliments like that. He was very supportive of my Olympic goal. He liked people with passion, who had a dream and a purpose in life. He liked my big ideas and my enthusiasm for life. He also liked to establish plans for his next races in Spain or abroad, looking for challenging adventures that had never been done before, or isolated locations that only a few trail runners would dare try. Yet at the same time, he was easy-going, an uncomplicated person.

At races, he used to always place on the podium, but after I arrived, he would run with me instead, at my slower pace. His friends made fun of him, but he never minded. They liked to call him *Abuelo*, "Grandpa." Salva would reply *"Ver mi culo!"* which means "See my ass!" because they were slower and couldn't catch him in a race.

He always said exactly what is on his mind. I sometimes tease him gently about it, calling him "Forrest Gump."

Later Salva and I were invited to race at Peneda-Gerês in Portugal with Carlos Sá Trail Adventure. It was my debut as a mountain racer and my first ultra-marathon in mountains, with four stages, over four days. The weather in early May was mostly heavy rain, wind, and freezing cold. Salva ran with me throughout the four stages. When the race was over, one of his friends posted a picture of us on Facebook, with the two of us holding hands as we crossed the finish line and the caption "Salva is now racing in the category of love," complete with the red heart emoticon. I was embarrassed for him, but he took it as a friendly joke. Salva was the only one among his friends who had stayed single, and had always vowed to them he'd stay romance-free. Yet here he was, having found someone who could make him forget the joy of carefree wandering!

#

As León became a new home for me, and I made new friends. A special one was Roberto.

During my first winter in Spain, Salva had to give two-day classes for the Winter Training Camp at the Aviva Sport Center in Ourense province, about 300 kilometers from León city. There would be about 20 students, with mixed levels of experience in mountain running. He would conduct theory and video conferences, as well as a few technical practice runs in the mountains. I went to assist Salva, and I noticed during the run a veteran couple who seemed to be lagging behind the group. I was concerned that they would get lost. I tried to let Salva know, but he said it was all right—Roberto and Pilar were here to enjoy the camp atmosphere rather than concentrating on their performance. We needn't be worried, because they knew the region well.

At the training, we ate at long tables in two rows with food in the middle of the table. Roberto was sitting on my left, and Salva at my right, while Roberto's wife, Pilar, was opposite him. Back then, I could understand a lot of Spanish but speak only a few words, so I tried to use simple French and English to communicate. Or sign language! Roberto connected with me best, in this same mix of languages. He surprised his wife by making me laugh.

At the end of the meal, Pilar told me that Roberto had advanced brain cancer. I felt a cold shiver, but at the same time a great admiration for his courage to continue living a normal life. From the beginning, Roberto and I felt a mutual respect and shared a joy of living.

When the training camp ended, we took pictures and exchanged contact details. In the following days, Roberto and I exchanged a lot of messages and became close. He told me that he had only three best friends, and I was one of them. I was surprised and honored. He shared his medical diagnosis with me, and his fear at having only a short time to live. Sometimes it felt like he knew me better than my own family did. I didn't tell him about my palm reading, and the prediction that I would die young, but I felt I could relate to his fear a little. It was truly a gift to have met him, and to be his friend.

When I ran my first mountain race at Peneda-Gerês, we got a wonderful surprise on day two: Roberto and Pilar were there at a checkpoint in the rain, cheering us on. We found them at the next checkpoint, and the next one, until the last day of the race. They had driven back and forth between Spain and Portugal just to support us because Roberto knew about my fear of running in the mountains. He and Pilar were completely soaked in the heavy, cold rain, but that didn't stop them. For me, that was an immense gift of love. I don't recall that anyone had ever demonstrated so much caring, protection, patience and love for me. I hoped that Roberto's health would remain stable, so that I would have time to get to know him further and share more stories with him.

#

But I did need to concentrate on my Olympic goals. If I was going to get into the Olympics, it had to be in 2016—waiting for another four years wasn't an option. After all, I was already 43 years old.

To strengthen my quest for a nomination, I would need to have run a marathon in under three hours. Salva and I had signed up in advance for two races in Spain in 2015: in Valencia on November 15, and three weeks later, in Castillon. Originally, Salva thought it would be better to aim for Castillon, to give us more time to train and make sure I was in perfect shape. But I wanted to run in Valencia, knowing that if I did well in an internationally renowned race like that one (as opposed to the lesser known Castillon), it would be easier to convince the Cambodian Government to nominate me, and easier to be accepted by the Olympic committee.

In the end, we agreed that I would run in Valencia, but I wouldn't go the whole distance if I didn't keep to the expected pace or if my hip injury started to act up. If either of these things happened, I would drop out at the 30-kilometer mark and try again at Castillon.

A few days before the race, I read on its website that there would be a "Valencia to Rio" prize. Any athlete who qualified for the Rio games based on his or her Valencia running time would be awarded €5,000.

Certainly that would help a lot in financing my road to the games, but I didn't sign up for it because I hadn't been in contact with the Cambodian government about the nomination yet, and I didn't yet know if I could run the race in under three hours.

We wanted to book a hotel room near the starting line, but so close to race day there weren't any available. Salva suggested that we stay at a vacation house owned by the parents of a long-term running friend, Ana. It was a 30-minute drive from the race.

I was not comfortable with this option. Before a race, I prefer to be alone and focused, and after a race I like to spend time with friends. Still, Ana's parents Herme and Pepe were adorable and generous, so we accepted their invitation. It was a seven-hour drive from León, and we arrived late on Friday night at the Tavernes de la Valldigna Platja village. Ana arrived the next morning from Madrid, and all five of us stayed in the very charming apartment with its view over the calm blue sea. Her parents brought crates from their farm full of freshly picked oranges, clementines and persimmons from which to prepare our morning juice. Herme grew up in Paris with her aunt, so she spoke to me in French about her past and how she met Pepe during her summer vacations in Valencia. Pepe was a big chef and concocted delicious traditional Valencia dishes, such as seafood paella for our carbo-load before the race.

I felt very grateful to be so warmly welcomed. They treated us like their own children, and their love for Ana made me dream of how it would have been if I'd had parents like them. At the same time, I thought of how lucky I was to meet all these wonderful people in a very short time. My life was now so different from what it had been in New York and Cambodia. In Spain, I had found a place where I finally felt serene.

Salva ran with me in the race, pacing me, carrying my energy food, and running to water stations to get me drinks if I needed them. I passed the halfway point of the marathon after only 1hr 27min, without any discomfort. I was excited and hopeful. I might run even better than the time we had planned.

Soon after that, one of the other runners slowly passed me. I sped up a little, too—after all, she wasn't going very much faster, and I was doing so well in the race. But Salva looked over at me, and gave me a jokey warning. "I see you! Don't follow her!"

Two or three kilometers later, we saw her pulled over to the side of the race with a cramp. Neither of us said anything, but our thoughts were the same: that could have been me.

I stuck to the plan for the rest of the race, and we passed several other athletes who had pulled to the side with cramps, injuries or dehydration.

I started to worry as we got closer to the finish line—a GPS device I was carrying was showing what I later found out was a slightly longer distance to the end than was true. I was worried that I would miss out on those last few precious seconds I needed to get under the three-hour barrier. I had to dig deeper within myself to find the motivation, my eyes always on the giant clock on the top of the finish arch. Those last 800 meters, racing against the seconds ticking away on that big clock, were the most scary and exhausting of the whole marathon.

I powered past the finish line—with a time of 2 hours, 59 minutes and 12 seconds! So in the end, it was a very good thing that I went to Valencia. Not only did I manage to lower my time below three hours, but the organizer was on the Olympic Committee, and could verify my time in person.

That day I felt ecstatic. I had passed the first hurdle to getting into the Olympic Games.

-16-
Getting Nominated for the Olympic Games

Unfortunately, top physical performance isn't all it takes to get to the Olympics. There's endless paperwork and bureaucracy. Step one would be to get nominated by the Cambodian government's Khmer Amateur Athletics Federation and the National Olympic Committee of Cambodia.

I was very aware that this was my last chance at the Olympics, but I didn't want to seek favors from my government or compromise my principles. I could make the argument that I was still a good candidate, even though I was four years older than when I'd been turned down for the London games—I was getting faster, not slower!

From my experience with the 2012 games, I knew how politics worked in Cambodia. It was mostly about people trying to get ahead, and not about doing the best thing for the country. I didn't want my own Olympic path to reflect that. I wanted it to be about inspiring Cambodia, about showing that we could stand with other countries on an equal footing. I knew I wasn't going to win, or even be on the podium, but I wanted to compete for Cambodia in this ultimate international setting.

First, I needed to convince Cambodian sport officials to use what's known as a "wild card" for me. Countries use these to send athletes even if they don't qualify strictly on merit. The idea is to encourage greater international participation in the games, especially developing countries. The qualifying standard time for the Rio marathon was 2 hours 19 minutes for males and 2 hours 45 minutes for females. We didn't have any runners with those times, but in the future, I believed, that could change. Having a Cambodian (me!) in the Olympic Marathon, I would argue, would help encourage the development of the sport in Cambodia. If I finished, I would be an inspiration for perseverance and a model for young women, showing that they could excel not only in academia, but in sport.

Previously, Cambodia had sent female competitors for the 100-meter race, but usually they never made it past the first qualification meet. I would argue that since there were no qualifying meets for the marathon, I would be guaranteed to be in the event. Cambodia would get television coverage, no matter what, which would benefit national pride. After that nasty dust-up with the Japanese comedian in the previous games, I just wasn't sure that officials would be interested in what I had to say. But I had to try.

Salva and I flew to Phnom Penh. I went in to see secretary general of the national Olympic committee, having rehearsed those strong and convincing arguments, but my nerves were twisted into knots! Salva was there by my side as my coach. I gave a heartfelt speech to the secretary general. My case was quite strong: I had come in four minutes below the time of the female gold medalist at the Southeast Asian Games of that year. Still, I expected him to ask questions and debate my points. But to my surprise, he listened closely, and when I finished, he said, "Yes. What do you need?"

I couldn't believe this meeting was going so well. I told him I needed an official nomination letter, and not just a verbal promise. The next stage would be to get approval at the global level, from the International Association of Athletics Federations and the International Olympic Committee.

Believe it or not, the Japanese-Cambodian comedian Neko was again coming into the picture. This time, however, things were much less in his favor in terms of a running record. His most recent recognized race was the Tokyo marathon two years earlier. However, the comedian had one thing I didn't have: money. I wanted to get into the games on my merit. I wouldn't bribe my way in, but there were still a lot of things that required money that I just didn't have: plane tickets, room and board at Iten, and a running outfit, to name a few.

Along with my official nomination letter, I received a letter from the committee requesting that I find a sponsor, preferably one that would be willing to sponsor the whole Cambodian team and delegation. This was very unusual—usually it was the duty of the government to find the money to support their Olympic athletes. I already had a lot to do to prepare, and now there was this as well!

There was this immensely tall, imposing Nigerian guy calling himself "Black Mamba" who had lived for a while in Cambodia and worked as an expert adviser at the national Olympic committee, aside from being a preacher in a religious group and having numerous other jobs in Phnom Penh. The job of drafting my committee letter fell to him, and he suggested that I take him on as my manager, in part to help me publicize my road to the games in order to get sponsors. I told him I would need first to see the type of contract he had in mind.

Later on, Black Mamba sent me a contract in which he would receive 30 percent of any financial sponsorship I could find. The deal and its complicated clauses smelled fishy. I declined his offer, telling him that Salva and I would do fine by ourselves.

At the same time, I contacted one of the youth race organizers, who was a businessman, politician, and friend of the prime minister's son. He immediately agreed to sponsor the whole cost of my Olympic training, saying it didn't matter how much I needed. I was cautious, and took Salva with me to several meetings that I had with him in Ta Khmau province, about 20 kilometers from Phnom Penh. From the beginning, I wanted to be honest and clear that I wouldn't be aligning myself with a political party nor get involved in advertising, say, any brand of alcoholic drinks. We had several late afternoon meetings at a coffee restaurant in Ta Khmau.

When it came time to confirm the sponsorship, though, it was a washout. The man ignored my calls and emails. I suspected that my chances ended when I said I wouldn't align with any party. But I will never know for sure.

Salva and I returned to León. I would fall back on my savings. But then people began coming forward not with a full sponsorship but portions of one. My running club Intelligent Interval provided my Olympic running outfit. Salva's physiotherapist Grupo Fisioclinicas offered free consultations and therapeutic massages. After I posted on my social media page that I was seeking sponsors, friends donated a couple of hundred dollars through PayPal.

Salva contacted the Valencia organizers about the "Valencia to Rio" program, with my national nomination details for the Olympics. The organizers kindly retroactively included my name on the list for the grant.

There was a sad development at this time, however. We had tried to get in touch with our friend Roberto, but got no response. Feeling that something was wrong, we reached out to his wife, Pilar. She confirmed what we had feared: Roberto's health had declined. He could barely talk, and was having trouble recognizing even his family members. He had been having chemotherapy, which left him sick for several days. He didn't like to see people in that state, so we respected that wish and stayed away.

Salva took five months off his job without pay to help me train and, to be at my side. It was all set now. I would run at the 2016 Rio Olympics, with Salva as my coach.

I would have to train my hardest, but make sure that I didn't get new injuries or exacerbate the hip injury I'd sustained earlier. I was having problems with an awful, itchy rash, which was especially bad at night and prevented me from sleeping. It usually started on my fingers and then progressed to the rest of my body. It had begun a few weeks before Valencia.

I checked with some dermatologists, but they didn't find any cause for it. Finally, they suggested that emotional stress might be behind the problem. It reminded me of when I had talked to my physiotherapist about a constant, intense tension in my right shoulder, and he'd said that that part of the body often corresponded to stressful parental relationships! At first I felt a bit cynical about his interpretation and smiled wryly to myself. I wanted a science-based diagnosis. As far as I was concerned, that sort of explanation just meant that they hadn't found the real reason and just wanted to tell me something to make me feel better.

But after both the physiotherapist and the dermatologists had talked about symptoms having a basis in emotions, I started to give those theories some credit. Even my hairdresser suggested that emotional stress might be the cause of some hair loss I was experiencing.

I decided to return to HATC to train, with Salva. It was, after all, known as the "Home of the Champions." On April 18, I arrived there for my third time; Salva was thrilled to have his first experience in Iten.

I began a very demanding regimen. A rare break came on June 6, my birthday, when I did only one run. I suggested that instead of receiving gifts, I would bring gifts to the children at a nearby school. We bought notebooks, pens, pencils, chalk, and some posters and sweets. It was a great day. We received plenty of adorable smiles and happy faces, and returned to HATC with our hearts full of joy.

But the day ended in sorrow. That afternoon, we got a message from Pilar. Roberto had lost his battle with cancer, before we'd had a chance to see him again. I felt shocked and pained and guilty. As one of his best friends, I should have been at his side holding his hand so he could leave this world in peace. I had only known him for a last year and a half, but I felt like I had lost a lifelong friend.

When the Olympic Games approached and I still hadn't found any formal sponsors, the mission chief of the National Olympic Committee of Cambodia said the organization would take care of my air tickets to Rio. The Cambodian delegation would be travelling as a group, at a cost of $4,000 each. The committee's secretary general agreed that I would fly from HATC to Spain, then to Rio for the games, and return from there to Cambodia as part of the official delegation. The mission chief got in touch with me to set the date of my flight to Rio, but he couldn't seem to find any seats on the days I needed.

Salva, meanwhile, was denied a pass to the games as my official coach, which meant he would have to pay everything himself. Even to get into the Olympic village to see me, he would have to obtain permission each time. Cambodia was sending a Khmer Amateur Athletics Federation representative as the official athletics coach. It was this person who would get the expenses and stay at the Olympic village. It was a very tough decision, but Salva decided that in view of the enormous cost and hassle, he wouldn't go to the Olympics at all. He would follow my journey by phone, on social media and on TV instead. It was painful for me to accept this, as we had been partners from the beginning on the road to the Olympic Games, but accept it I did.

By now there were just three weeks to go. Every day I was out on the trails of Iten. Salva was my partner, my coach. He and my Kenyan pacers Ben and Joseph kept me in constant motion: "You can make it! The finish line is just around the corner!" These were their constant refrains. I was physically and mentally exhausted by the training, yet I had also to give constant interviews to journalists, with requests for more interviews in Rio.

The opening ceremony of the games was drawing ever closer, but I still didn't have my air ticket, the costs of which were skyrocketing. Finally, with Salva's help, I found a ticket. Instead of going directly to Rio from Spain, I would go to Porto, Portugal, and then on to Rio. It would save the Cambodian committee more than $1,200 on the ticket cost, but it meant I would arrive in Rio only twelve hours before the opening ceremony.

I sent my ticket request to the mission chief, but to my shock, he made excuses about why they couldn't buy the ticket. It would be better, I was told, if I bought the ticket myself, and the committee would reimburse me after I sent the receipt. I had a feeling that this would go badly. It wasn't just the money. It was that people were always trying to use their positions of power for their own benefit. It was disgraceful and disrespectful. I hadn't requested financial help from Cambodian committee for my training in León or Iten. I used my own means, while some other Cambodian athletes received grants for their training abroad. Here I was, the first female Cambodian Olympic marathon runner, and they were trying to cheat me out of my airfare.

The more I thought about it, the more I recalled other times when people had taken advantage of my trust and good intentions. I worried that my stress was going to leave me in bad shape for the Olympics. I was losing sleep over money and sponsorship, which only increased my rash.

I went ahead and bought the ticket, and in the end, I was right to be suspicious. After the mission chief received the receipt, he informed the financial department that they could only refund me for the cost from Rio to Cambodia, when I would be traveling with the delegation—not the ticket to get there. They were only going to pay me back for half the expense. So I decided to write a short account of my situation to the committee's secretary general, and I copied in the mission chief. I also shared the email with a Cambodian friend who was minister of tourism and knew the president of the committee.

I was so offended by how I was being treated that I was privately contemplating a "Plan B." If I didn't get a full reimbursement, the only way I could think of to demonstrate my discontent would be to go to Rio but not take the start line at the marathon. I would publically denounce to the media the Cambodian committee's refusal to support their own athletes. I'd get in trouble with the government, for certain, but I was ready to take the risk because I was so revolted.

Thankfully, they gave in. Less than 48 hours after I sent the email and talked to my friend, I got a full reimbursement. I would run in the Olympic Games after all.

#

As I prepared to leave for Rio, I set three goals for myself.

First, I would be on the starting line of the Olympic marathon. I wanted the world to see a Cambodian athlete there, equal to all the other competitors.

Second, I would finish the race. The position in which I would finish was not a priority, even if I came in dead last. I would persevere to the end and cross the finish line to prove that even at my age I could do it and inspire other Cambodian women to do even better in the future.

Third, I would run a personal best. I had trained to achieve a target of 2 hours 50 minutes. A personal best would be the cherry on top of the whole experience. It would be testimony that commitment and willpower can allow us to achieve our potential.

A quote from Pierre de Coubertin kept going through my head: "The most important thing in the Olympic Games is not to win but to take part, just as the most important thing in life is not the triumph but the struggle. The essential thing is not to have conquered, but to have fought well."

-17-
Summer Olympics:
26 Miles in the Blazing Heat of Rio

Just because I'd managed to get the plane tickets didn't mean everything went smoothly. My flight from Madrid to Porto was cancelled an hour before it was supposed to depart. It was a mess—the passengers were all angry, and Salva had already left the airport after dropping me off. I borrowed another passenger's mobile phone to call him, so he could help me figure out what to do.

Finally, after hours of waiting at the airport, the Portuguese airline TAP put me on a priority flight, as I was an Olympian who had to be in Rio for the Opening Ceremony no matter what. They found me a seat on a flight from Madrid to Recife, north of Brazil, where I would have to spend a few hours overnighting at a hotel before taking another flight to Rio. Needless to say, that night in Recife I barely slept. But, the final flight left on schedule, putting me in Rio in the early afternoon. I had only four hours to get into the city, find the Cambodian delegation and officials, give a quick interview for Cambodian news, then put on my uniform, a stylish yet traditional purple silk dress, for the Opening Ceremony.

As I marched into the stadium behind the Cambodian flag, I felt enormous pride to be representing my country. The stadium was huge; the lights and projected beams were overwhelming; the ambience was electric; every color was on display; the cacophony of sounds was thunderous; the weather was stifling. I felt disorientated and yet in wonderment! Every one of my senses was being assaulted. All this, and the anticipation of what I was actually there to do -- to run the race of my life. I felt goose bumps of emotion and exhaustion all at once.

#

The "village" at each Olympic games is a place where all athletes stay together and concentrate on preparing for their events. The village in Rio housed 11,231 athletes representing 207 nations from every corner of the world. There were countries I had never heard of. The village was like a miniature world all to itself—everyone was speaking different languages, wearing different kinds of clothes. There was an alley with all the participating countries' flags hanging on display, and there were flags over the buildings and windows, too. The atmosphere was extraordinary—just to think that we had all made it here for the same purpose: to live together in peace for a few days or weeks, and to represent our countries with dignity and pride through fair competition.

For the first time, the IOC had created a Refugee Olympic Team, athletes who'd experienced daunting adversities and overcome fight and displacement to emerge strong and become Olympians. I was touched, of course, in view of my own past. I talked with several members of the Refugee Olympic Team from Africa. We exchanged Olympic pins and took selfies together. The whole experience gave me hope for humanity.

Ever since the terrorist attack at the 1972 games in Germany, there has been extremely high security at all Olympic villages. At Rio, you needed your personal badge to get in and out. Armed military guards were on the lookout at each corner and building. Rio wanted to make sure that we were very safe. If we had to train outside, vehicles with guards took us there.

If you had any medical needs, all sorts of professionals were available: sports injury specialists, of course, but even dentists. There were parks and tennis courts, a gym, media rooms, restaurants, conference rooms and meeting halls, shops, and a post office. There was plenty of entertainment, too: animations, music and dance.

I'd like to say that my home country's politics didn't follow me to Rio, but they did. I was supposed to share a room with a Cambodian girl who was competing in Taekwondo. Cambodia hoped she would win a medal, since she'd won gold at the Southeast Asian Games. They called her the "golden girl." She had received major financial support. She had been the flag-bearer at the opening ceremony, and many political leaders had come to support her.

I can't know why, but at the last minute, she was assigned a whole room to herself. I got an unfinished closet as a bedroom. It didn't have screens on the windows to keep the bugs out, only a mosquito net. (The games took place during a time of fear about the Zika virus epidemic. The Olympic Village was sprayed with insecticide daily.)

#

After the Opening Ceremony, there were nine days to go before my race. I kept busy with daily training, physiotherapy, media interviews, and helping out as an interpreter for Cambodian officials. One day we got on a bus and went out to see the course I'd be running.

Then it was Sunday, August 14. The day of the race.

I had set an alarm clock for 4:00 a.m. and a second for 4:15 as backup. I wanted to have plenty time to get ready and catch a 6:30 a.m. bus from the Olympic village to Sambódromo stadium, where the race would begin. Of course, I didn't need the clocks. After a fitful night, reliving past marathons in my head, I woke up on my own.

Shortly after, my mobile phone rang. It was Salva calling to check that I was awake and wish me luck. That day, he was also going to run a race: the Villalfeide mountain race, organized by a friend of ours. The timing was perfect: he would be able to finish his race then go to our friend's house to watch mine on TV.

As I readied myself to leave for the stadium, I kept telling myself: *this is it.* All the hard work and sacrifice that you've endured—now is the time to put them to work.

At Sambódromo stadium, athletes, coaches and medical teams entered a cordoned-off open space which was set up with tents, tables and chairs. In the middle was a warm-up area of synthetic grass. Each country's team grabbed a spot to put down their stuff. I was impressed at how well organized and sophisticated some of the teams were. Such equipment they'd brought: massage tables, giant coolers. Coaches were preparing the athletes' T-shirts and pinning on their bib number.

I didn't need to get dressed, however, since the first thing I'd done after my shower at the village was to put on my shirt and bib number. I started to warm up on the synthetic green. Some of the runners were lying on the ground to relax. Others were getting last-minute messages and pep talks from their coaches. At this moment I missed Salva.

I kept repeating to myself: Everything is fine! Don't worry! In three hours, it will be done!

Then, a smiling athlete, Catherine Bertone from Italy, approached me, asking if she had it right about my name and age. I was surprised that she knew so much about me. She said she was happy to see me, that we had been born in the same year. I understood. We were the two oldest runners! She asked her coach to take a picture of us together. After we compared our exact dates of birth, we had a good laugh, because I was the younger by three months. Olympic media reporters had erred in saying that I was the oldest athlete in the female marathon.

So here it was, the day I'd worked so hard for—the day that a Cambodian woman would line up at the Olympic marathon, equal to the athletes from other countries. Standing under the start arch toward at the back of the group, I tried to relax, thinking of good things and reassuring myself that my training had been good, that only positive things would happen as long as I reached the finish line. I rehearsed in my mind the pace I needed to keep throughout the race to reach my goal of 2 hours 50 minutes—or anything under 2 hours 59 minutes, my personal best. I was asking my guardian angels—those same benevolent spirits to whom I'd prayed as a Cambodian child—to keep me safe along the way. I just kept repeating the mantra: Everything is fine! In three hours, you'll be finished!

Then, against official announcements, blaring music and the cheering of the joyful crowd, I heard the start of the countdown. It was 9:30 a.m. and so far not too hot—73 degrees Fahrenheit, 23 Centigrade.

The gun went off.

#

My legs began moving. I tried to keep to my own pace and not get carried off by the faster speed of certain other runners as they started. I soon settled into the pack of runners as I'd planned.

Around the second kilometer, one of the runners pulled over to the side. It seemed she was dropping out. I knew that could be me. Even though I'd never dropped out of a race, the thought was very much on my mind. I just kept reciting my mantra. Everything is fine! Don't worry! In three hours, it will be done!

On the other side of the world, in front of a TV screen, Salva and his friends were thrilled at the sight, proud to have a friend running the Olympic marathon. They watched me pass the 5k mark. The people in front of the TV included some who'd never showed interest in the Olympics; now they were totally engrossed.

Everything was going to plan—until K7. There I started to feel a sharp pain in my right Achilles tendon. In the days before, my physiotherapist at the Olympic village had noticed extreme tension in my calves and proposed taping my ankles for the race, but I refused, thinking I would be fine.

What a misfortune this was —and so early in the race. My mind conjured up scenarios in which the pain grew progressively worse with each additional kilometer. I was frightened, yet I managed to take this setback in stride, so to speak. Keeping up my pace, I revised my running plan in my head. With an injured tendon, I wouldn't be able to achieve a personal best. I would just try to cross the finish line.

The temperature was already edging up. The air was very humid. We were running on asphalt, which made the heat worse. Along the raceway, the organizers had installed artificial showers imitating a fine rain and water sponges to cool us down and prevent heatstroke. There were bottles of water too. I grabbed a few and poured them over my head as I ran. I should have been more careful. Water running down my body got into my socks and before long was creating blisters on my feet. This added to the pain from my Achilles tendon. Still, I kept going.

The course included three 10-kilometer laps along the beach before returning to the finish line. All along the course, huge crowds were cheering warmly from behind security barricades. As I passed, they chanted "Cambodia! Cambodia!" Some were biking or running along the barricade, taking selfies and videos. I greeted them in return, giving high fives, waving to people at the top of a bridge and blowing kisses. With every lap, the crowd got crazier and more excited, screaming louder and louder. At one end of the U-turn area, people were in absolute delirium, lifting their hands in the air as I passed, doing the wave! I got very emotional, receiving so much love from strangers from different nations, all calling my name—"Ly!"—just as it was written on my bib— or "Go Cambodia!" I couldn't hold back my tears. I cried as I ran. I forgot about the pain in my tendon, and the blisters on my feet, and my exhaustion from the heat. I passed other runners who had dropped out. My heart went out to them, but the sight also gave me new strength to avoid ending my race that way.

By Kilometer 35, I was falling behind the pack. Just before passing the loop of the last lap, a Singaporean overtook me, but I still wasn't in last place. Soon enough, though, the Saudi runner, who had finished last in the London Olympics, overtook me too, and this left me last. When she passed, we cheered each other along. She went ahead; I was now in the company of the motorcycle rearguards.

Over in Spain, Salva was having trouble following me. Though TV channels in many countries followed the race through the awards ceremony, the one that Salva was watching cut off at about 2 hours 35 minutes, shortly after, the TV channel suddenly cut off transmission after a Kenyan runner, Jemima Sumgong, won the race, and the last remaining Spanish runner reached the finish. Desperately frustrated, Salva jumped in his car and rushed home to watch on the Internet, hoping he would make it in time to see me cross the finish line.

It was noon now. I had only seven kilometers to go. I felt like I was in a toaster—heat coming down from the sky above and up from the asphalt below. Negative thoughts arose in my mind, even though I tried to stay focused. Behind me I could hear motorcycles revving their engines. A helicopter was hovering above my head. It was intimidating—were they frustrated that I wasn't running faster? But I was going as fast as I could! My legs were numb and my ankle ached. My GPS seemed to take an eternity to pop for each completed kilometer. My legs got heavier and heavier.

I thought of everyone who had gotten me to this point—of Salva, who had coached me and lived my Olympic adventure, of the people in Kenya who had paced me, of my French mother, who had taken in a girl who had no one.

I was so close to my goal! Only five kilometers left!

I needed extra energy, extreme determination and resolve to face the final straight. I had to reach beyond what I was capable of physically, emotionally and psychologically. I needed to find a force within myself that I'd never tapped, a second wind of inner strength.

I started to think of my life journey, my perseverance and determination in the face of adversity. All through those years, I was able to find strength to complete tasks that some might regard as crazy or hopeless. Now I had a new challenge: I had to keep going, to fulfil my promise to myself to bring love and pride in the Olympic arena for my country, which had suffered, persevered and survived, despite the misery that history had dealt up for it.

In Spain, Salva was starting to grow desperate. He had expected me to finish at 2 hours 50 minutes, but it was now past the third hour and he couldn't see my name among the finishers. Had I been injured? Had I dropped out? Was I in the hospital? The minutes kept ticking by, 3 hours 5 minutes, 3 hours 10 minutes. All the while, messages from friends and family were pouring in demanding to know how I'd done and what my time was. He had seen other finishers collapse from heat exhaustion and dehydration, then be carried off on stretchers for medical help. The suspense was unbearable.

Somehow I was still running. The sun was crazy-hot. I could barely feel my legs—except for the jab of pain from my Achilles tendon every time my right foot hit the ground. That was nothing compared to what I was going through emotionally. During the last two kilometers, I started to doubt I would reach the finish line. I considered pulling over to surrender to the pain and the exhaustion. Then I remembered my persistent dream of helping my country and making Cambodia proud. This now depended on me. It would all have been in vain if I quit—I was the only female marathon runner ever to represent Cambodia. Pulling over just wasn't an option! I told myself, "Just keep pushing!" My pain was nothing compared to what my country and I would lose if I gave up.

I remembered the speed work I had done in Iten with Salva and my Kenyan pacers Ben and Joseph. I heard their encouragement: "You can make it! The finish line is just around the corner!"

I gathered all those memories of suffering, misery, and painful childhood separations. Many times I was lost and in despair, but I always found a way to persevere. People do not have to remain miserable or lost! I peppered myself with self-talk as fuel to push me forward a little bit closer to the finishing arch. The most important thing was to keep the motion of my legs going.

Then it was true—just as Salva and my pacers had told me. I turned the last corner, and the finish line was in sight! The crowd started to stand up and cheer! I thought to myself, "This is it. It's only a few hundred meters until the end, and I'll have won my fight!" The greatest sense of satisfaction and gratification swept over me: I had found a way to make it to the end.

By now, I could sense that the cheering had spread to people on both sides of the avenue to Sambódromo stadium. True, I was the last runner, but they were calling out their respect and admiration to me, and through me to the Cambodian nation. I ran toward the finish in harmony with this loving crowd. I kept my head up all the way, embracing the spectators' acclamation. Suddenly my spirit was light and peaceful, though physically I was ready to fall flat at the finish arch.

Suddenly, I spotted a volunteer straight ahead, thrusting something red and blue at me. It was a Cambodian flag! In the background, I heard the Bruce Springsteen song "Glory Days."

I grabbed the flag and unfolded it, holding it up over my head with pride. After 3 hours 20 minutes and 20 seconds I crossed the finish line under the shadow of my country's flag. I felt pure bliss! This was the greatest moment of my life; I was living a dream. I was a strong woman and an Olympian marathon finisher!

With the flag now wrapped around my sweaty body, I gave greetings and respect to the people around me, using the traditional Khmer gesture of sampeah, placing both my palms together in front of me in a position of prayer. I had crossed the finish line; 24 women who began the race did not.

#

Twice in my life, I had been told that I would die young. Now it didn't seem to matter anymore. I was happy. Finally, I wouldn't mind dying.

It was more than having achieved a personal goal of running in the Olympics. As I trudged away from the finish line, I felt that all my past struggle was worth it. I had worked hard to acquire scientific expertise and improve health care in my destitute homeland. Now I'd helped bring the Cambodian nation, once broken, a feeling of happiness and pride to compete with other nations in this Olympic arena. Cambodia had sent a runner who crossed the finish line in a race that about one in five competitors were unable to complete. It was proof positive that we could pick ourselves up from hard times and wear our scars like a badge of honour.

When I arrived back at the Olympic village, I was limping severely. I could barely put my right foot on the ground. I put maximum weight on my left leg and dragged myself toward the restaurant to grab some electrolyte drinks and food. A shuttle bus took me to my building. At last, I reached my private space, where I iced my swollen Achilles tendon and tried to eat something. Then I called the other side of the world to update Salva. My tears were flowing, and my nose was running. Physically and emotionally exhausted, I was barely able to explain the race experience and my emotions. But what bliss it was to hear Salva's cheerful voice. He'd made it to his Internet link in time. He described his immense joy at seeing me on the screen for the last straight, smiling brightly, as always, and waving to everyone in the crowd. For him, knowing that I had reached the finish safely was more important than the time. We were simply ecstatic that I had made it through.

I spent the last couple of days in Rio reading messages on my phone and crying over them. There were too many to count, from friends, from family, from people I'd never met, from people who had read articles about me, or watched me run, and who were proud of me and my accomplishment. There were people who said I was inspiring, people who said they had doubted me, but I had proved them wrong, people who said that I had done something amazing both for myself and for Cambodia. My sister Heang told me that I had brought honor and pride to our family. Her kids' friends were sharing messages, pictures and videos on social media. I recalled the bitter moments when I wished that I could have heard from people during my rough road to the Olympic Games! Now I cried by realizing what an amazing gift it was to be able to make other people happy and proud, not just myself. These messages and a one minute and thirty seconds video from the finish line were the best souvenirs I could have from my time at the Olympics.

From HATC in Kenya, Peter told me that I got more screen time more than the actual winners of the race. So, he said, I was the real winner. My French mother saw me featured in the "best picture" and "best story" segments on the day of my race. Probably millions more saw those segments, broadcast in countries around the world. Articles and interviews with me were copied, translated and spread from country to country.

#

Then it was time to go home. I limped onto the bus to head to the airport. I flew to Phnom Penh, where we had a press conference with the minister of education and sport and local journalists, followed by a dinner of congratulation. Cambodian officials and coaches took the floor after the Taekwondo "golden girl" (she'd been eliminated in her first round of competition) gave her impressions. I spoke too. I said that in the future we should use an Olympics wild card for another marathoner rather than a 100-meter sprinter because the impact was bigger and the feat more inspirational, even if we couldn't make the podium. We all received a bouquet and sports outfit with the colors of the Cambodian flag.

A few weeks later, I was back in Spain. I was still unable to walk properly. Salva took me to see Javier, the physiotherapist at the Grupo Fisioclinicas. An ultrasound produced an image showing my tendon was about to break. The right Achilles was in a very abnormal crescent shape.

A full month and a half passed before I was finally able to jog slowly. But even mild pressure on my Achilles still brought pain. I got three weeks of intensive treatment with the painful Intratissue Percutaneous

Electrolysis (EPI) to boost the healing of the soft tissue. I also got collagen growth factor injections around the tendon to stimulate the growth of new ligament and tendon tissue. Javier prescribed rehabilitation exercises. A full eight months would pass before I was able to resume my training. Even now, at the time of this writing, a residual pain persists. I regard this pain to be my Olympic Games scar!

That October, maman came to León to visit Salva and me. She went mountain hiking, met my Spanish friends, saw the historic sites, and returned home with her luggage full of León delicacies. I was learning that family sentiment is based on caring for each other—on love, not blood.

There was one thing, though, that I truly regretted about my Olympic Games experience. I regretted that Roberto hadn't lived to see it, and that I had not been able to make the time for a final visit with him.

But I had done it. I had run across the finish line as Cambodia's first female Olympic long-distance runner. I had accomplished my dream.

-18-
Life After the Olympics

Back in Cambodia, some of the old botherations resumed. I went to the National Sport Center to get my national athlete's salary, but for some reason it was not available. Constant delays and complicated issues followed, but, out of principle, I didn't want to let anyone else get what was due to me. I hoped I would set a precedent for future national athletes getting the respect they deserved.

The expert advisor for the national Olympic committee tried to claim a share of my salary for doing his job, but I told him politely that I was sorry, I wouldn't give him that share. I kept contacting and contacting again until I finally received the last of the salary in February 2017, more than six months after the games.

During my last training in Iten, there were rumors about doping among young Kenyan runners who were just below the top international times, including a few at Iten. Star runners were said to be using erythropoietin (EPO) to enhance their performance. A few months later, the first Kenyan woman to win Gold at an Olympic marathon was confirmed positive for doping and banned for four years. It wasn't the first such ban, and it wouldn't be the last. I couldn't help feeling deeply disappointed in these athletes, meant to be an inspiration to young and old. To me, it was against everything the Olympic games were about.

In November 2017, Sothéa Phal, a young French-Cambodian male runner, and I organized two Keyla Torsu (Sporting Perseverance) teams, with six runners in each team, for the Paris Ekiden relay. This was meant to be a sort of symbol of us passing the torch to a younger Cambodian generation, for them to become the next Olympians.

#

I had accomplished my own promise to honor people of my nation once broken, but I still had a life to live. I continued to teach at the

University of Health in Phnom Penh. I would have to come up with new plans and projects, ones that would include Salva as well.

These days I still race regularly. I get regular invitations to enter international races in Singapore and Thailand as a Cambodian elite runner. I go, but I don't prepare with an intense training program, nor do I plan my entire life around running.

Salva and I are happy to live simply in Spain. We are renovating a house in Peñalba de Santiago. We will have our own vegetable garden and be beekeepers. Being together enjoying nature brings us happiness, and Salva's job earns us enough to live.

Now that I have the time to reflect upon my life, I realize that I was brought up without a role model. Under the Khmer Rouge, we were taught to suppress our emotions, so I never learned how to express, identify and manage personal feelings. I believe that this lack of love in my childhood caused some physiological stress disorders.

I have also started to accept that I am both fortunate and unfortunate at the same time. The circumstances of my birth were unfortunate: beginning life so close to the Khmer Rouge time and being taken from my Cambodian family. At the same time, I was fortunate to be able to go to France and have the opportunities I did there. I am lucky too that I had a resilient mindset, followed my heart and intuition, and constantly worked hard, looking for courage to confront the most brutal realities. Otherwise I might have started using drugs and alcohol.

Writing the story of my life helped me achieve a sense of peace and equilibrium. But, as I mentioned at the start of this story, finding the right words to express my pain was harder than I thought.

I was also concerned about self-disclosure, whether it would be safe to talk about my life story and my private feelings. I felt vulnerable knowing that I would be sharing so much with complete strangers. Yet I hoped that doing so would contribute to the growth of others. My intent is that my story will be meaningful for other Cambodians who are survivors, not necessarily of the Khmer Rouge times but of any seemingly impossible challenge. I came to believe it is my responsibility to see this writing project through, to motivate people who are going through hard times and, I hope, inspire younger generations.

I began to realize, too, the value of being able to move on. Back when I was living with my foster family, I thought a lot about taking revenge on Ludovic and others who humiliated me or took advantage of my naivety. Nowadays, things are different. The best revenge is taking no revenge but focusing on moving forward. I'm truly happy to see that my foster mother is open-minded to change. She has shared her emotions with me, which has made our relationship much better. Now we are able to laugh about our old conflicts.

People often ask me "Where are you from?" It's a hard question to answer. I am a native Cambodian but I have been educated in many places throughout the world. Sometimes I am asked, "Where do you call home?" This question is even harder. Home can be anywhere I feel emotionally connected, welcomed and loved for being me. If home is where the heart is, Spain is where it is at this time. But, truly, the more open and flexible I am in life, the blurrier the location of "home" becomes. I have learned to adapt and live freely, so home truly can be anywhere.

#

With the Olympics behind me, I've been lucky to have many opportunities to spread my message. I've been asked to be a godmother for an annual race in León to support scientific research on infantile cancer at the Vall d'Hebron Research Institute in Barcelona. I've spoken at a World Health Organization conference about my life, both in terms of HIV research and athletics. I have been interviewed by Singaporean TV as an inspirational athlete. In Phnom Penh, I've talked at Lycée Descartes (the French high school) and the Australian International School. I share my experiences and try to provide a positive contribution to people's personal growth. Whenever I travel, I use some of my free time to volunteer. I am happy to now have a flexible schedule to contribute, to give back at my own pace and in my own way.

One of my favorite talks took place in a Léon public school. The children there were studying developing countries. I introduced them to my life, and to the trials and wonders of the country of Cambodia. One 10-year-old boy asked his teacher if he could write my story. He did; I was honored to be his protagonist. But this was not a standard schoolboy's assignment. When he had finished writing his piece, it was included in a book—Historias del Mundo—Somos Uno (Stories of the World—We are One) that the school assembled and published. At a promotion event for the book in Ponce de León College, I was enchanted to be at his side as he read his work in front of classmates, parents, and other spectators.

Once again I couldn't hold back my tears. It was a reminder that life can be simple and beautiful. And oh what a blessing it is to be able to inspire others.

-Epilogue-

There was once a young lotus shoot. It was the last to spring from its cluster in the shallow, muddy pond during the monsoon. That year, a great tropical storm blew in. The sky went dark, heavy clouds hurried through lightning and thunder. A strong wind blew furiously. It turned into a full typhoon, the most powerful storm the area had ever endured. It dumped torrential rain on the lotus pond.

In a short time, the winds broke many of the lotus shoots that had grown tall already. They floated away, swirling in turbulent waters. The young lotus shoot was too small to be broken, however, and it was part of a lucky cluster that came to rest in a lake far downstream. Its roots went down into the mud, and soon it blossomed into a beautiful lotus flower.

Across Asia, the lotus is an important symbol, appearing in Buddhist, Hindu, Sikh and Confucian imagery and philosophy. It is a symbol of purity, because it is a beautiful, perfect flower that grows out of mud and draws sustenance from sunlight.

No one among us is perfect and pure like the young lotus. But I hope that this memoir, recounted as best I could, will serve as an inspiration for others who find themselves facing a great typhoon in life.

October 2006: At University of Bordeaux 2, France. My PhD jury members.

December 2006: At the International Angkor Wat Half marathon, Siem Reap.
Crossing the finish line of my first race.

May 2015: At Peneda-Gerês multiple stage race, in Portugal. *With Roberto at a checkpoint under a heavy cold rain where Pilar and Roberto came to cheer us.*

November 2015: Finish line at Valencia marathon, Spain. Breaking the mythical barrier of 3h with a new personal best of 2h59'12".

June 6, 2016: For my birthday we brought gifts to the children of Somongi school, in exchange we received plenty of sparkling smiles from kids.

-Acknowledgments-

I would like to express my deepest appreciation to Lee Cope for helping shape my autobiography.

Many times I was unsure if I would publish this book. I'm ever thankful for encouragement to proceed from Salvador Calvo Redondo, who has always been at my side to support my projects, from my foster mother, who took me in when I was a child, and from many friends who encouraged me to share my story with the world.

Thanks to Momoe Takeuchi who saw the promise in my book and gave me special counsel to tell it sooner rather than later.

My sincerest thanks go to my editor John Burgess, who gave valuable guidance to make this book better, and to my friends Catherine Hiller, Pierre Fallavier and Jill Hamill for providing their sincere critiques, suggestions and support.

I'm especially grateful to my León friends, the Grupo Fisioclínicas, the Intelligent Interval School, and the worldwide running community for their friendship and warm cheering on my road to the Olympics.

-Note-

Some names in this book were changed or presented without surnames in order to preserve privacy.

-About the author-

Nary Ly is Cambodia's first female Olympic marathoner. A survivor of the Khmer Rouge genocide of the 1970s, she holds a PhD in biology and medical sciences. She speaks widely about her life journey in hopes of inspiring personal achievement in others who face adversity.